10 TRUE TALES

VIETNAM WAR HEROES

By Allan Zullo

SCHOLASTIC INC.

To all the brave men and women who served in the Vietnam War, especially those who gave their lives for our country.

—A.Z.

Copyright © 2014 by The Wordsellers, Inc.

All rights reserved. Published by Scholastic Inc., *Publishers since 1920*. SCHOLASTIC and associated logos are trademarks and/or registered trademarks of Scholastic Inc.

The publisher does not have any control over and does not assume any responsibility for author or third-party websites or their content.

No part of this publication may be reproduced, stored in a retrieval system, or transmitted in any form or by any means, electronic, mechanical, photocopying, recording, or otherwise, without written permission of the publisher. For information regarding permission, write to Scholastic Inc., Attention: Permissions Department, 557 Broadway, New York, NY 10012.

ISBN 978-0-545-83750-7

10 9 8 7 6 5 4 3 2 1   15 16 17 18 19

Printed in the U.S.A.   40
This edition first printing 2015

ACKNOWLEDGMENTS

I wish to thank all the former servicemen featured in the following pages for their willingness to share, in personal interviews with me, the dramatic and sometimes emotional memories of their combat experiences from decades ago.

This book was made better by the full cooperation of the Congressional Medal of Honor Society, especially Carol Cepregi, the society's deputy director of operations. She was instrumental in helping me select the heroes and paving the way for my interviews. For all of Ms. Cepregi's efforts, I am extremely grateful. I also thank the society's archivist, Laura Jowdy.

My appreciation extends to those who provided me additional information and confirmation of certain facts. They include: Chinta Strausberg, Jim Stanford, Yvette Garcia, and John Levitow, Jr.

AUTHOR'S NOTE

After writing *World War II Heroes*; *War Heroes: Voices from Iraq*; and *Battle Heroes: Voices from Afghanistan*, I felt a duty to spotlight another band of brothers — the courageous members of the United States military who served so valiantly in the Vietnam War.

An estimated 1.6 million members of the Army, Navy, Air Force, and Marines experienced, or were exposed to, combat at some point in the 1960s and 1970s in a hostile country halfway around the world. There's an important story about every person who served in this war. Because it's not possible to write about each one, I've chosen to highlight the stories of ten heroes — soldiers, Marines, and airmen who received the Medal of Honor for their daring actions in Vietnam.

The medal is America's highest military honor and is awarded by the president of the United States for personal acts of valor above and beyond the call of duty and at the risk of one's life.

"True courage is very rare," President Lyndon Johnson said back in 1966 when he presented the award post-humously to Private First Class Milton Olive III, whose gripping but tragic story is told in this book. "This honor we reserve for the most courageous of all of our sons. The Medal of Honor . . . is bestowed for courage demonstrated not in blindly overlooking danger, but in meeting it with eyes clearly open."

The heroes in this book would be the first to tell you that they proudly wear the medal not for their own glory, but for all the men and women who fought for the United States.

"Even though we each were singled out for a specific action, we wear that ribbon for all those who served in Vietnam," says Harold "Hal" Fritz. He was an Army lieutenant who showed unbelievable bravery when he and his wounded 28-member unit held off 200 enemy soldiers in an ambush.

Speaking about his fellow Medal of Honor recipients, James Livingston, a Marine captain who fought in an exhausting three-day battle against overwhelming odds, says, "None of us consider ourselves real heroes, because we survived. We wear the awards for those Marines and sailors who did not make it home. Those are the people we honor, and it is a sacred and honored privilege to wear the award in their names. Receiving it is a great distinction, but also humbling, because other good fellows died, and we are the witnesses to their actions and bravery. We are the holders of their history and legacy."

For this book, I reviewed battle accounts and military citations. Then I conducted lengthy personal interviews with the selected heroes and asked them to relive the heart-stopping moments that earned them their medals for valor. Three of the stories feature heroes who have passed away. I gathered information about them from their family members, news accounts, transcriptions of interviews they had given before their deaths, and, in one case, an autobiography.

When you read the gripping accounts of the bold actions of all the heroes in this book, you'll see that they displayed a tenacity that spurred them to reach far beyond their personal limits. Some found within themselves an incredible courage that they didn't even know they had.

Their stories are written as factual and truthful versions of their recollections, although some of the dialogue has been re-created. Because there are so many military terms used in these accounts, there is a glossary at the back of the book.

Americans in uniform deserve our respect, our support, and our gratitude. This book is a salute to their courage, honor, and gallantry.

— Allan Zullo

CONTENTS

THE VIETNAM WAR

The Vietnam War was an armed conflict involving communist North Vietnam and local guerrilla fighters known as the Viet Cong who fought against South Vietnam and its main ally, the United States, in the 1960s and 1970s.

This war in Southeast Asia started long before the U.S. sent troops into battle. In the 1950s, the country was split between North Vietnam — headed by President and Prime Minister Ho Chi Minh of the communist Viet Minh party — and South Vietnam, ruled by American-backed Ngo Dinh Diem. When Diem refused to hold elections to unify the country, the Viet Cong (called the VC for short) launched a guerrilla war against the South with major combat help from the North Vietnam Army (NVA).

THE VIETNAM WAR

Many in the United States feared that if South Vietnam fell to communism, other nearby Southeast Asian countries such as Laos, Cambodia, and Thailand would also end up communist. This theory was called the "domino effect." As a result, in the early 1960s, President John F. Kennedy sent money and American military advisers to help the South Vietnamese forces, known as the Army of the Republic of Vietnam (ARVN).

In February 1965, after the Viet Cong attacked American air bases and killed American soldiers, President Lyndon Johnson retaliated by ordering regular bombing raids (code-named Operation Rolling Thunder) and sending the first U.S. ground troops into battle. Johnson said his goal was to help the ARVN defeat the Viet Cong and the NVA, who were supported by communist countries China and the Soviet Union.

While American planes bombed North Vietnam — including its capital, Hanoi — U.S. troops fought a jungle war in South Vietnam. Infantrymen slogged across flooded rice paddies, hacked their way through dense jungle, and trekked along booby-trapped paths. They fought in stifling heat, monsoon rains, and gooey mud against an enemy that fired from "spider holes" and hidden bunkers and escaped through a complex network of underground tunnels.

Among the local peasants and villagers, American ground troops had a hard time determining friend from foe. Many of the Vietnamese — including children and old women — acted as spies, laid booby traps, conducted sabotage, and fed and housed the VC.

Those Americans who served in-country also had to deal with scorpions, snakes, mosquitoes, and leeches as well as malaria, dysentery, dehydration, and "jungle rot" — various skin conditions caused by the tropical climate.

In the majority of battles, helicopter crews braved rocket-propelled grenades, machine guns, and automatic-weapons fire to drop off soldiers, pick up the wounded and dead, and lay down covering fire for the ground troops. Crews on Navy gunboats and patrol boats on Vietnam's narrow, twisting rivers faced much the same dangers. Air Force pilots were dogged by surface-to-air missiles, antiaircraft weapons, and Russian-built fighter jets known as MiGs.

Because the VC often hid in the dense jungles, U.S. planes tried to destroy their cover by spraying Agent Orange, a toxic chemical that killed vegetation, and by dropping napalm, a fiery bomb that burned and cleared any targeted area.

Millions of refugees poured into camps near the South Vietnam capital of Saigon and other cities because their homes were in areas that had been declared "free-fire zones." These zones were created to isolate the VC and NVA soldiers and were cleared by the military of innocent civilians, so that anyone left behind was considered an enemy combatant.

By April 1969 American combat troop strength topped out at 543,000. About 25 percent of the troops were draftees —

able-bodied young men who were required to join the military whether they wanted to or not.

Back home, public opinion began turning against the war after appalling images of maimed soldiers and civilians were broadcast on the nightly news. Antiwar protests, marches, and gatherings spread across the United States. On November 15, 1969, in the largest antiwar demonstration in our country's history, more than 250,000 Americans descended on Washington, D.C., demanding the withdrawal of U.S. troops in Vietnam. The antiwar movement, which flourished on college campuses, bitterly divided the United States. Many Americans felt the war was a pointless, unwinnable political conflict that was costing the U.S. too much in casualties and money, not to mention the suffering endured by innocent Vietnamese civilians. However, many other Americans — what President Richard Nixon termed "the silent majority" — had a different view. They thought the war was necessary to stop the spread of communism, believed in their country "right or wrong," strongly supported the troops, and accused protestors of being unpatriotic traitors whose actions gave comfort to the enemy.

By 1970, the United States began slowly withdrawing American troops while increasing aerial and artillery bombardment. The military also started turning control of ground operations over to the South Vietnamese.

In January 1973, the United States and North Vietnam finally reached a peace agreement, ending open hostilities between the two nations. However, war between North and South Vietnam continued until April 30, 1975, when NVA forces captured Saigon and renamed it Ho Chi Minh City. The following year, North and South became one communist country — the Socialist Republic of Vietnam.

People in the country who helped the American military or were connected to the South Vietnamese government were severely punished by the new communist regime. Many had their homes and businesses taken away; tens of thousands were shipped to camps for "reeducation" or sent to work on farms; others were imprisoned or executed. Persecution and poverty spurred an estimated two million "boat people" to flee from Vietnam in fishing vessels.

Despite the communist takeover of Vietnam, no other country in Southeast Asia fell to communism other than its neighbor Laos. Supporters of the war contend that it was precisely because of America's involvement that the domino effect was prevented. After a series of economic and political reforms that began in 1986, Vietnam and the United States resumed diplomatic and trade relations in 1995. Today, the country has a growing economy and tourism industry.

The war was a costly one for America in terms of human suffering: Of the 1.6 million men and women who fought or were exposed to combat in Vietnam at some point during the war, more than 58,200 were killed, 61 percent of whom were 21 years or younger. More than 150,000 of the 304,000 who were wounded required hospitalization; half these patients were severely disabled. An estimated 700 to 800 were held as prisoners of war and tortured; more than 100 were killed or died during captivity. Today more than 1,600 Americans are still missing in action in Southeast Asia, including nearly 1,300 in Vietnam.

The government of Vietnam claims as many as 2 million civilians on both sides and 1.1 million North Vietnamese and Viet Cong fighters were killed. The U.S. military estimates that as many as 250,000 South Vietnamese soldiers died in the war.

Even though American troops fought with just as much tenacity, determination, and valor as those in previous conflicts, many returning Vietnam War vets didn't get the recognition they deserved back home because of the controversial nature of the conflict. Critics on both sides of the political spectrum blamed the politicians in Washington for interfering with military operations and setting bad U.S. policy. Unfortunately and unfairly, the returning vets caught much of the flak for the unpopular war. But, over time, the vast majority of Americans came to recognize the incredible sacrifices and valiant deeds of these brave vets. Ever since its dedication in 1982, the Vietnam Veterans Memorial and its signature monument — The Wall, which displays the names of every known serviceman and servicewoman who gave his or her life — stands as a somber testament to duty for our country. It is the most visited site in our nation's capital.

Regardless of the differing views of the Vietnam War, there's one thing that everyone can agree on: The men and women of the United States military served there with guts and grit.

"WE WILL NEVER GIVE UP!"
Army Lieutenant Harold "Hal" Fritz

It seemed hopeless.

Twenty-eight soldiers — all but five badly wounded or dead in the first few minutes of a devastating ambush — were trying to fend off a force of two hundred NVA soldiers who were battering the Americans from two sides with RPGs (rocket-propelled grenades), grenades, and small arms fire.

Trapped on a road outside their burning armored vehicles, a platoon from the Blackhorse Regiment was on the verge of being overwhelmed and overrun. They knew their only chance of survival — however slim — rested on the shoulders of their tough, strong-willed leader, Lieutenant Harold "Hal" Fritz.

Ignoring the blood and pain from a shrapnel wound to his back, Fritz kept running from vehicle to vehicle, positioning his men, assisting the wounded, distributing ammunition, and directing fire for the few who were still able to shoot a weapon. "We will never give up!" he shouted to his men. They believed him. With Fritz exposed in front while he manned a machine gun, the soldiers thwarted the swarming enemy's first direct attack. But when a second wave of NVA soldiers gathered for another thrust, the gutsy officer thought, *We have to do something so unexpected, so unbelievable, and so outrageous that it creates mass confusion and terror in the enemy.*

That's when he came up with an idea that was beyond drastic, beyond crazy. But there were no other options. It was do or die.

Hal Fritz did not know the meaning of the word *quit*. Eight months earlier, on May 18, 1968, he had cemented his reputation as a ferocious warrior who could make smart, quick decisions in the heat of battle. He was serving as tank platoon leader with Company D, 1st Squadron, 11th Armored Cavalry Regiment (known as the Blackhorse Regiment) during a fierce battle with a well-entrenched NVA battalion. While leading his platoon on several assaults, Fritz personally destroyed numerous bunkers. When he ran out of ammunition for his machine gun, he threw it down and picked up an automatic weapon that he fired with deadly accuracy until it malfunctioned. Then, with complete disregard for his safety, he repeatedly exposed himself to enemy fire, hurling hand grenades until he was wounded by shrapnel from an enemy rocket. Ordered to the rear, Fritz refused medical attention and instead began supervising the evacuation of other wounded personnel, including his commander. Despite his painful injuries, Fritz mounted a tank and rejoined the battle, fighting valiantly until the enemy was defeated. His heroic efforts earned him a Silver Star, one of the military's highest combat medals.

Throughout the rest of the year, his battle skills were tested repeatedly — and he always passed. But on this day, January 11, 1969, on this deadly stretch of road, he was facing the ultimate challenge that tested not only his abilities as an officer but his very being.

Just days from ending his tour of duty, Fritz — who was now the executive officer of the Blackhorse Regiment's Troop A, 1st Squadron — had volunteered to lead a unit of heavily armored vehicles on a sweep of a crucial stretch of Highway 13, looking for signs of the enemy. The mostly unpaved road was a vital route where large truck convoys carried ammunition, clothing, aviation fuel, diesel, food, and other supplies to American forces. These twice-a-week convoys were prime targets for hit-and-run ambushes by the NVA, especially in an area known as Thunder 3 in Binh Long Province.

That morning, Fritz had headed out with 28 men in seven ACAVs (armored cavalry assault vehicles) that moved on their own set of continuous tracks, similar to a tank. Six of the vehicles had two M60 machine guns on either side of the rear hatch and a .50-caliber machine gun, all with protective metal shields. The seventh vehicle, the Vulcan, looked much like the others, except it had a rapid-fire 20-mm cannon mounted on a turret that could swivel 360 degrees and was designed to shoot down low-flying aircraft.

After scouting Thunder 3 up to the village of An Loc without incident, the unit turned around and headed partway back. At about 10:30 A.M., they were getting into a position at a specific spot — near where a sniper had taken a few potshots earlier — to wait for the approaching 125-truck convoy, which was about 20 kilometers away. Most of the troops, including Fritz, were sitting on top of their vehicles.

Although Fritz was concentrating on his mission, swirling in the back of his head was the happy thought that he was scheduled to leave Vietnam within a few days and soon would be embracing his wife, Mary, and baby back in Wisconsin.

Suddenly, Fritz's ACAV, which was behind the lead vehicle, was rocked by a powerful explosion. The force threw him to the ground and sent hot shrapnel ripping into his back. The stunned officer scrambled to his feet, thinking his now-burning vehicle had struck a land mine. He climbed back on top and discovered that his two gunners were dead, the M60s were blown off, and the .50-caliber machine gun was inoperable. He knew then that the vehicle had been hit by an RPG.

Fritz surveyed the scene quickly and saw that several of the ACAVs were on fire and disabled, his men trapped in a well-orchestrated ambush. A large group of NVA soldiers was shooting at the Americans from one side of the road while another enemy unit was firing up from a lower railroad embankment on the opposite side of the road.

As flames licked at his heels, Fritz stood on top of his burning vehicle and used hand signals to get his men repositioned. Then he jumped down and went from vehicle to vehicle to see who was injured and who could fight. Things looked grim: Two were dead and about twenty were wounded. Some of the smoldering ACAVs were exploding after flames had reached the ammunition stored inside them.

Everything bad was happening at lightning speed. *We need to return fire as quickly as possible,* Fritz thought. He jumped off and ordered those who were able-bodied to bring the wounded up toward the front. Then he directed fire for those who could shoot — including several of the wounded. The enemy was so close that the Americans couldn't use the machine guns mounted on the vehicles because the weapons couldn't be aimed that low.

A new soldier who was inside the lead ACAV when it got hit was in shock and didn't move, even though his vehicle was on fire. Fritz pulled him out and threw him on the ground. Shoving an M16 into the soldier's hand, Fritz said, "Show me some firepower!" The soldier snapped out of his mental paralysis and started blasting away.

We need to send out a warning for the convoy coming up the road to stop so they won't run into the ambush, Fritz thought. He reached inside a burning vehicle and grabbed the mike only to discover that the cord was no longer attached to the radio. It didn't matter. The radio was destroyed anyway. *Oh, great. No communication.*

Fritz picked up an M60 machine gun and began firing it until he ran out of ammo. Then he pulled out his .45-caliber pistol and kept shooting that.

Meanwhile, Sergeant Don Larson was on top of his vehicle, firing his .50-caliber machine gun nonstop until the barrel of the weapon got so hot it began to melt and spew bullets in a spiral-like pattern. Specialist 5th Class Brett Tuttle, who was wounded when an RPG struck his vehicle, was hustling from one side of the ACAV to the other, mowing down the enemy with his machine gun. Together they and other soldiers in the front of the line of ACAVs had silenced three RPG teams and stalled the enemy from advancing. Tuttle and Larson weren't supposed to be here. They had done their time in-country and were scheduled to catch a flight home. But because Fritz had been short of people on this day, they had volunteered to go on one last mission.

The firefight was the first combat experience for the unit's medic, Specialist 4th Class Herbert Fabian. Even though he was a newbie, he didn't act like one. Reacting instantly and disregarding his own safety, Fabian was often fully exposed to the enemy while administering first aid to his wounded comrades and moving them to cover. Time after time, he had to stop working on a soldier and instead pick up a machine gun and lay down suppressive fire.

After fellow trooper George Rodriguez was shot, Fabian began treating him. Minutes later, Fabian looked up at Fritz, shook his head, and put his thumbs down. It was a signal that Rodriguez wasn't going to survive.

I'm not willing to lose another man, Fritz thought. He ran over to Rodriguez, kneeled down, grabbed the flak jacket of the barely conscious soldier, and shook him. Rodriguez opened one eye. Fritz then uttered the first thing that came to his mind: "George, do you know what we need right now?"

The bleeding man murmured a weak, "What?"

"We need a nice cold Coca-Cola."

Rodriguez opened his other eye and gave Fritz a look of befuddlement as if to say, "What are you talking about?" When Fabian saw that Rodriguez was still responsive, he began administering aid to him again.

By now, everyone was hurt, many so seriously that only five could still fight. In addition to getting injured in the back, Fritz had wounds to his head, shoulder, and chest. One comrade came over to Fritz and said, "Man, you're a bloody mess." Fritz was too charged up to feel much pain. Besides, he didn't have time to think of himself. His priority was to save his men. *Keep going, keep going, keep going!* he told himself repeatedly. *If I get shot and killed, the next guy will take over.*

Fritz believed the first 30 seconds of an ambush usually determined who would end up the victor. He figured if he and his men could return effective fire within 30 seconds — which they did — they might have a chance. Even though the Americans were taking casualties and were in a vulnerable position, they were putting up a spirited defense, using the smoke and flames from their burning ACAVs as cover. Surprised by the Americans' quick response, the enemy tried ground assaults, first from one side of the 25-foot-wide road and then from the other. But Fritz and his men repelled them.

Somehow we're going to get out of this, he thought. It was more than just wishful thinking. The mere fact that the Americans had withstood the initial onslaught had boosted their confidence.

They had patched up a radio, using parts from other damaged radios, but it was destroyed by an enemy bullet while they were sending a transmission. Now they had no way of knowing whether their warning to the convoy and plea for reinforcements were heard.

"I don't know how long we can hold them," Fritz told Tuttle. "There's no way we can e-and-e [escape and evade] them, because they have us surrounded. We have to hold them back as best we can until help comes. If it comes."

"WE WILL NEVER GIVE UP!"

At one point during the frenzied battle, Fritz experienced the weirdest sensation of his life: He felt himself leave his body. The entire firefight became subdued — even the sounds. Everyone and everything moved in slow motion, including the tracer bullets that seemed to float past him. It was as if he was watching the battle rather than fighting in it. Then his life unfolded in front of him. He saw himself as a boy growing up in Lake Geneva, Wisconsin, with dreams of becoming a veterinarian; then as a married part-time college student running a family business; then as a 22-year-old draftee enlisting in the Army, graduating from Officer Candidate School, and being deployed to Vietnam. Then . . . *Bang! Bang! Bang!* . . . Fritz returned to real time in the pitched firefight.

Whatever fear he felt, whatever emotional turmoil was bubbling inside him, the lieutenant didn't show it. He was too consumed with protecting his men and slaying his enemies. Fear would have to wait before it could be felt. Right now he needed his men to trust in him, to give him 110 percent, to never hesitate. They did. And they believed him when he shouted, "We will never give up!" *This won't be a repeat of Custer's Last Stand,* he told himself.

After 30 minutes of fending off the enemy, Fritz decided it was time to go on the offensive and do something so extreme and outlandish that it would send the enemy into a tailspin. His audacious idea: He and the few men who could still fight would charge their foes.

"WE WILL NEVER GIVE UP!"

"If we charge them, they won't know how to react," he told his comrades. "They won't be expecting it. We have to act so ferociously that they'll cower. This can work."

Leaving Fabian back to protect the wounded and prevent an attack from the other side of the road, Fritz and three others prepared for their assault. As much as they believed in him, he believed in his men, who had been fighting with uncommon courage and valor. He looked into their eyes and saw their fury over the ambush and rage over the deaths of their two brothers. *If we don't make it, at least we will have died gloriously on the battlefield,* he thought.

With his pistol in one hand and a bayonet in the other, Fritz led his men in the daring charge. Yelling and screaming like maniacs, they sprinted toward the startled NVA force. Stabbing enemy soldiers in hand-to-hand combat and shooting them at point-blank range, the Americans sent the North Vietnamese reeling.

After a quick thrust, Fritz and the soldiers raced back to their wounded comrades before the enemy on the other side of the road had a chance to overrun them. After catching his breath, he told his men, "If it worked once, it can work again." So then Fritz led another charge.

This time he encountered the biggest enemy soldier he had ever seen. Wielding an AK-47 with a bayonet, the foe was moving toward Fritz from two meters away. Fritz aimed his pistol at the man's chest and pulled the trigger. It went *click*. At the same time, the enemy soldier pointed his assault rifle at Fritz and pulled the trigger. Incredibly, it went *click*, too. Given a reprieve from certain death, Fritz grabbed the barrel of the AK-47, wrestled it away from his foe, and stabbed him.

The second charge was as effective as the first one, although Fritz knew that their forceful action bought them only a little time. The small unit had held off an estimated 200 NVA soldiers for nearly an hour, but the Americans were running out of ammo and energy. Without reinforcements, they were doomed against the large, well-trained, well-equipped NVA force.

Now it was the enemy's turn to charge. Foes rushed onto the road and engaged in close-in combat. While he fought back, Fritz saw a cloud of dust down the road. Poking through the top of the swirling haze was the black, red, and white Blackhorse Regiment flag and an antenna. It was the lead vehicle of H Company, a tank platoon. *They came just in time,* he thought. But then he noticed that the tanks had stopped about 150 meters away. *Why aren't they moving? We're getting hammered here.*

"Something is wrong," Fritz told Larson. "I don't know why they aren't coming, and I can't talk to them because we still don't have radio contact. I have to go get them."

Despite being fully exposed, Fritz began running down the road as bullets zinged past him with every stride. Nearing the lead tank, he saw its big gun swivel toward him and then fire. The muzzle blast blew him eight meters backward off the road and into the bushes. Fortunately, he didn't get hit with any shell fragments, but he momentarily lost his hearing. After he crawled out of the brush, Fritz, whose ears were still ringing, scrambled to his feet and ran up to the tank commander, Lieutenant Jim Caldwell, and yelled, "Why did you shoot at me?"

"Sorry, Fritz," Caldwell replied. "There was a sapper team behind you, and they were about to fire an RPG at us. We had to take them out."

"Why have you stopped?"

"We can't tell the difference between you guys and the bad guys through all the smoke because everyone is covered in red dust," Caldwell replied. "We're trying to figure out what to do next and where to go."

Using hand signals, Fritz deployed the tanks, which quickly moved into position and were soon joined by two infantry companies from the 1st Cavalry Division. As Fritz ran back to join his comrades, he knew the Americans would soon rout the enemy, which they did.

After reinforcements came in and the wounded were being evacuated, Larson pointed to the new troops and told Fritz, "We didn't need those guys. We had the enemy on the ropes."

"Do you know what the odds were against us?" Fritz replied.

"Yeah, but we had 'em beat."

"WE WILL NEVER GIVE UP!"

Even though his uniform was soaked with his blood and painful wounds were sapping his strength, Fritz refused to be medevacked until all his other men were helicopter out. He and Tuttle were the last men in the platoon to leave the area as the reinforcements continued to engage in sporadic combat.

At the hospital, Fritz examined the bullet holes and shrapnel tears in his uniform. For the first time that day a wave of fear swept over him from the reality of just how close he had been to being killed. But then he shook off that uneasy feeling. In fact, he was determined to return to the battlefield.

As the medical staff cut off the men's tattered uniforms and treated their wounds, Fritz told Tuttle, "We've got to get back there."

"How are we going to do that?" asked Tuttle.

"You steal some clothes, I'll get the weapons and a vehicle, and we'll drive back there."

"Sounds like a plan."

While Tuttle found some doctor's scrubs, Fritz swiped two guns. Then he located an unattended Jeep that had a red cross painted on its canvas top and another on its hood. He knew it was against the Geneva Convention to use an ambulance or medical vehicle for combat. So he removed the canvas and covered the red cross on the hood with mud.

Fritz and Tuttle hopped into the Jeep, returned to the scene of the ambush, and helped the reinforcements capture and kill several NVA troops who hadn't retreated. The rest of his wounded men all survived.

Shortly after arriving back at their base, Fritz received a phone call from Colonel George Patton, son of the famous World War II general of the same name. "I heard from the hospital in An Loc that there were two wounded soldiers who went AWOL and that a Jeep and some weapons are missing," Patton said. "I put two and two together and came up with Fritz. Get the Jeep and weapons back to the hospital ASAP!"

At the end of the firefight, a soldier had picked up a damaged cigarette lighter that he found lying on the battlefield. It had been struck by a bullet. Engraved on the lighter were Fritz's name and the words, "With love, Mary." His wife, Mary, had given it to him before he was deployed to Vietnam, telling him, "Think of me whenever you use it. I hope it brings you good luck because you need to return alive."

Thankful to have the lighter back, Fritz told the soldier, "I always kept it in my left breast pocket over my heart. I lost it during the battle when I got hit in the chest. The lighter deflected the bullet, but the impact threw me off the vehicle. If the lighter hadn't been in my pocket, I'd be dead. I guess that means it just wasn't my time yet."

Fritz's belief that fate or a higher power had a hand in his survival was further confirmed shortly after he returned to base. He tested the two weapons that had failed to work in the life-and-death confrontation between him and the big

NVA soldier during the Americans' second charge at the enemy. In the test, Fritz fired 100 rounds from both his .45-caliber pistol and his foe's AK-47 . . . and neither had a single malfunction.

For his remarkable actions during the heat of battle on that memorable January day in 1969, Harold Fritz was awarded the Medal of Honor by President Richard Nixon during a ceremony at the White House on March 2, 1971.

Fritz remained in the Army, serving 27 years before retiring as a lieutenant colonel. The father of four and grandfather of nine, Fritz lives in Peoria, Illinois, with his wife, Mary. He works in veterans' affairs and is also the current president of the Congressional Medal of Honor Society.

"That medal means I am representing the service and sacrifice of men and women who had served and lost their lives to protect the freedom of those in this country," Fritz says. "That ribbon and medal is not mine. It belongs to all the people who had served and made that sacrifice."

Brett Tuttle, Don Larson, and Herbert Fabian earned Silver Stars — the third-highest military award for valor during combat — in recognition of their courageous efforts that same day.

THE WILD WEASEL
Air Force Major Leo Thorsness

Leo, we got a launch! We got a launch!" shouted Captain Harry Johnson in the backseat of the Air Force F-105 fighter jet. "SAM at ten o'clock!"

In the pilot's seat, Major Leo Thorsness stared out the left side of the cockpit and spotted a North Vietnamese surface-to-air missile known as a SAM. Looking like a fat telephone pole with fire spewing out the back end, the guided missile was streaking straight toward them.

Referring to the call sign of the pilots of three other F-105s who were flying in formation with him, Thorsness radioed, "Cadillac, take it down!"

From an altitude of 18,000 feet, Thorsness rolled his plane inverted, plugged in the afterburner — a device that provides extra thrust — and pushed the nose nearly straight down. His fellow pilots did the same thing. But the deadly SAM followed them in their speedy descent. As the planes shrieked toward the ground at 600 miles an hour, life suddenly became simple for Thorsness: Don't crash and don't let the SAM hit you.

The ground loomed closer and closer. Two thousand feet . . . 1,500 feet . . . 1,000 feet . . . At the last second, he shouted, "Pull!" In unison, the planes pulled out of their death-defying dive, leveling off just above the treetops. But the SAM couldn't maneuver nearly as quickly and slammed into the ground in a fiery explosion.

Tracing the contrail — the trail of condensed water vapor that the SAM left behind — Thorsness and his team discovered the location of the missile launch site and bombed it into oblivion.

It was another success for Thorsness and his Wild Weasels.

Two search-and-destroy Wild Weasels were assigned to each F-105 squadron after the Soviet Union began supplying the North Vietnamese with SAMs. The Weasels would tempt the enemy into revealing the location of camouflaged missile sites and antiaircraft installations by deliberately getting targeted on radar. Because the F-105s had sophisticated electronic gear, they were able to detect the enemy's radar signals and trace them back to the source to locate the sites. The Weasels then wiped them out with air-to-ground missiles or bombs, clearing the way for a strike force of F-105 bombers to annihilate other targets.

Besides offering themselves up as bait, the Weasels faced several dangers. SAMs typically had a range of 17 miles compared to the F-105s' missiles of only 7 miles, so the enemy got to shoot first. Constantly harassing the Weasels were MiG fighter jets that were built for air-to-air combat and had much greater maneuverability. The one advantage the F-105s had was speed. When the afterburners kicked in, the jets could soar across the sky at supersonic speeds, leaving the slower MiGs far behind.

As a major and jet fighter pilot who had been in the Air Force for more than 15 years, Thorsness was "Head Weasel" of the 357th Tactical Fighter Squadron at Takhli Air Base in Thailand. Johnson, his electronics warfare officer (EWO) in the backseat, was in charge of detecting the enemy radar sites.

On April 19, 1967, on their 87th mission together over Vietnam, the pair took off in a plane with the call sign Kingfish 1. Joining them in formation were wingman Kingfish 2 (Major Tom Madison, pilot, and Captain Tom Sterling, the EWO) and two other planes, Kingfish 3 and 4. The four F-105s flew in advance of a bomber squadron on a mission to destroy an army barracks and storage supply facility near the heavily defended city of Hanoi, the capital of North Vietnam. When the Weasels were about 80 miles away, Johnson told Thorsness, "It's going to be a busy day. Already two SAM sites are looking at us with radar, and there are bound to be more."

About 25 miles from the target area, Thorsness directed Kingfish 3 and 4 to fly north while Kingfish 1 and 2 stayed south, forcing enemy gunners to divide their attention. Johnson reported that four SAM sites, plus several anti-aircraft installations, were now tracking them. Minutes later, Kingfish 1 and 2 fired their missiles and destroyed their first targets.

But then Kingfish 3 and Kingfish 4 radioed that they were being attacked by MiGs. Usually, in that situation, the F-105 pilots turned on their afterburners and outran the enemy. But Kingfish 4's afterburner failed. After several tense moments, the two skillful pilots were able to evade the MiGs and leave the area.

Kingfish 1 and 2 continued on their mission and bombed another SAM site. But then Thorsness heard Madison radio, "Kingfish 1, Kingfish 2 is hit!"

"Kingfish 2, head southeast toward the hills," Thorsness ordered. "Keep transmitting and I'll home in on you."

Madison radioed back, "I've got more warning cockpit lights!" Seconds later, he shouted, "It's getting worse!"

The next thing Thorsness heard over his radio was the sound of two beepers. It meant that Madison and Sterling had ejected from their crippled aircraft and deployed their parachutes, which automatically activated the beepers. He soon spotted the two chutes floating toward the foothills. Knowing that two fellow aviators had been shot down caused the major's stomach to twist in a knot.

"Leo, we got a MiG, low, nine o'clock!" Johnson announced. "There he is going under us right now. See him?"

"Yep," Thorsness replied. "He's setting up for a strafing run on Madison and Sterling. Harry, keep your eyes peeled. I'm going to try to take out that MiG."

"Have at him!"

Just as Thorsness had hoped, the enemy pilot was so focused on killing the two Americans in their parachutes that he didn't know Kingfish 1 had maneuvered behind him. Thorsness squeezed the trigger of his 20-mm cannon and watched the enemy's left wing break apart. As the MiG spiraled to its demise, the major shouted, "Harry, we got him!" It was the first time he had blown a plane out of the sky.

But the pilot's thrill vanished when Johnson warned, "Leo, we've got MiGs on our tail!"

The major looked behind him and saw one of the MiGs about 1,000 feet away. *If that pilot is a good one, we're dead,* Thorsness thought. Putting Kingfish 1 in a dive to the right, Thorsness turned on the afterburner while the MiG blasted away. But none of the bullets found their mark. Kingfish 1 was able to zoom off at 700 miles an hour, causing the slower MiG to give up.

Thorsness and Johnson flew over the mountains west of Hanoi and out of range of SAMs or MiGs. Having shot their missile, dropped their bombs, and fired their 20-mm cannon, the two Americans were low on ammo and fuel. They headed toward the closest refueling tanker, which was circling over northern Laos.

Thorsness radioed to the airborne command post the location where Madison and Sterling were last seen, triggering a search-and-rescue mission. The command post called up two A1E-Skyraiders (nicknamed Sandy) and a helicopter. The Sandy — a single-seat, propeller-driven World War II–era aircraft — was often used for rescue operations. The pilot's job was to make contact with the downed aviators, strafe enemy troops to prevent them from capturing the Americans, and direct the rescue helicopter to pick them up. For this particular mission, the Sandy pilots, who had never been attacked by MiGs or seen a SAM, had to fly closer to Hanoi than ever before.

As Kingfish 1 neared the tanker for refueling, Thorsness radioed each Sandy, "Be on your toes when you get close to the bail-out area. There are MiGs in the area, and you'll be within SAM range."

After refueling, Thorsness fretted about the two downed aviators and each Sandy because there were no other American planes to provide cover for them. *Without cover, chances are those guys on the ground will be captured or killed, and the Sandies are vulnerable,* he thought. *They need help.* Crossing his mind was a paraphrased quote he remembered reading from Hillel the Elder, the famous Jewish religious leader: "If not me, who? If not now, when?"

"Harry," he said on the intercom. "We need to go back. But if we do, we go it alone. And you know the odds aren't in our favor. Are you comfortable with that?"

"Let's go," Harry replied. "It's us or nobody."

So even though Kingfish 1 had little ammunition left, it turned around and headed for North Vietnam. Thorsness again tried to reach Madison and Sterling on a special radio channel. After his third attempt, he picked up a weak static-filled transmission and heard a voice so garbled he couldn't tell if it was speaking English or Vietnamese. He was aware that the enemy sometimes used Americans' survival kit emergency radios to trick rescue planes into flying into range of ambush-waiting MiGs.

"Leo! MiG at eight o'clock!" Johnson shouted.

The major spotted the enemy jet and another one at eleven o'clock and then three more. The MiGs were flying in a wide circle, known as a wagon wheel formation, over the bail-out area, poised to pick off any American plane during the rescue attempt.

Thorsness flew his F-105 right into the wagon wheel. Locking in on one of the MiGs in front of him, he fired the last rounds from his cannon. The final burst tore into the MiG, and Thorsness saw parts coming off the enemy plane, giving him a probable kill. Before the other enemy jets could attack Kingfish 1, he flipped on the afterburner and outdistanced them.

Once he was in the clear, he turned the plane around and headed back toward the bail-out area. Soon he heard a frantic voice on the radio from Sandy 2: "Sandy 1 is going in! Sandy 1 is going in! The MiGs got him! Oh, he just crashed into the side of a mountain!"

Thorsness radioed to Sandy 2, "Go as low and slow as you can and turn hard so the MiGs can't get you." Thorsness knew that because the MiGs were much faster than the Sandy, they couldn't make tight turns the way the Sandy could. "Keep your mike button down and keep talking so we can home in on you."

"Copy that," replied Sandy 2. "But hurry. There are at least four MiGs here."

As Thorsness's plane screeched low at 690 miles an hour, he wondered, *We have no missile and we have no ammo. What are we going to do when we get there?*

Moments later, he spotted three MiGs. Thinking fast, he decided to bluff them like a crafty poker player. *They don't know we're out of ammo,* he thought. *I have to make them believe I'm trying to shoot them down so maybe they'll turn their attention away from the Sandy and concentrate on trying to kill us.* It was a risky gamble, but he figured it was his best play.

Thorsness maneuvered Kingfish 1 between two MiGs in

a way he hoped would trick the enemy into thinking he didn't know which plane to attack first. The ruse worked to perfection. Sensing that the American pilot was confused and would make an easy target, the MiGs broke away from Sandy 2 and set their sights on downing Kingfish 1. That allowed Sandy 2 to slip out through a valley at treetop level to escape safely. (The rescue helicopter never arrived.)

Meanwhile, Thorsness was engaged in a deadly game of aerial tag with the MiGs. Once he knew that Sandy 2 was out of sight, he put on the afterburner and weaved through the mountains, outracing the MiGs. The satisfaction he felt over helping Sandy 2 escape was overshadowed by his great disappointment that the rescue attempt had failed. He tried calling Madison and Sterling on their emergency radios again, but there was no response.

Because he was critically low on fuel after dodging the MiGs, Thorsness radioed the tanker that was flying over Laos to set up a rendezvous. Their conversation was interrupted when a desperate F-105 pilot broke in and said he had only a few minutes left of fuel and needed the tanker. The pilot, whose call sign was Panda 4, was part of a four-plane strike flight that had been scrambled after Kingfish 1 left the bail-out area. They had engaged in a tense dogfight with the MiGs and shot two of them down. During the air battle, Panda 4 had become separated and lost.

Thorsness immediately understood the dilemma that they were all in: Panda 4 and Kingfish 1 were many miles apart from each other and extremely low on fuel. The tanker could only service one of them in time . . . but which one? If Kingfish 1 didn't get refueled, Thorsness and Johnson would have to attempt to fly 100 miles across enemy-occupied Laos and over the Mekong River to Thailand, an American ally.

"If we don't get fuel, there's a chance we can still go beyond the Mekong before flaming out, and then we could eject over friendly territory," Thorsness told Johnson. "But if Panda 4 doesn't get the fuel, he will have to eject over enemy territory."

"That's an easy choice," Johnson replied.

"Yep, the tanker belongs to Panda 4," said Thorsness. He radioed, "Tanker 1, you have six minutes to rendezvous with Panda 4, or he'll have to eject."

"Roger, Kingfish 1, we'll do our best."

Thorsness climbed to 35,000 feet where the air was thinner, allowing for better mileage of what little fuel was left in the tanks. Minutes later, he was pleased to learn that Panda 4 had successfully linked up with the tanker in the nick of time.

On the way toward Thailand, Thorsness remained devastated over the shootdown of Madison and Sterling. Ever since he had taken over as head of the Wild Weasels, he had promised himself never to lose a wingman in combat. And for 86 missions, it had never happened until now. He wondered, *Are they dead or alive? Have they been captured? What will I write to their wives?*

Thorsness contacted Udorn Air Base in Thailand, which was 130 miles from their present position, and alerted them to Kingfish 1's situation. Landing at Udorn was the two aviators' goal and best-case scenario. But they were prepared for the likelihood that they would be forced to eject somewhere near the Mekong — either in friendly or enemy territory, depending on which side of the river they would be when they ran out of fuel.

Thorsness did the math: *The F-105 can glide two miles for every 1,000 feet it drops. We're at 35,000 feet. If we can keep the engine running long enough, then we can glide for 70 miles and into friendly territory even if we have to eject before reaching Udorn.* When they were over Laos at 35,000 feet and 70 miles from the Mekong, he pulled the throttle to idle to save the last few precious drops of fuel and began gliding in a descent at 310 miles an hour. *If we don't make it, we'll either end up dead or a prisoner.*

Fifteen nerve-racking minutes later, Kingfish 1 coasted over the Mekong. At least they had made it into Thailand. Now the question was: Could they reach Udorn, which was 26 miles south of the Mekong? Luck was on their side. Even though the fuel gauge indicated empty, the engine kept running. Just as the plane touched down at Udorn, the engine shut down, out of fuel.

In the previous stress-filled hours, Thorsness and Johnson had destroyed two targets, shot down two enemy planes, prevented Madison and Sterling from being killed in their parachutes, helped save Panda 4's plane, and nursed their own fuel-starved jet to a safe landing.

In a classic understatement, Johnson told Thorsness, "Well, that was a full day's work."

Eleven days later, on April 30 — their 93rd mission — Thorsness was thinking of his wife, Gaylee, and 11-year-old daughter, Dawn, because pilots who completed 100 missions were sent home. *Only seven more missions to go,* he thought. *Maybe I can make it home for Mother's Day.*

Nearing their target, Thorsness and Johnson zoomed 690 miles an hour over a 10,000-foot mountain peak 70 miles west of Hanoi. They hadn't noticed the two MiGs that had been circling in the valley below. Suddenly, the aviators heard a loud warning signal in the cockpit, indicating that an enemy air-to-air missile was closing in on them from behind.

Seconds later, the plane shook violently, as if smacked by a giant sledgehammer. The controls no longer worked and the cockpit filled with smoke. An Atoll heat-seeking missile had just struck their jet right in the tailpipe.

Although the maximum speed for safely ejecting from an F-105 was 525 miles an hour, there was no time to slow the plane down because it was breaking apart. "Go!" shouted Thorsness, ejecting a second after Johnson did.

Catapulted into the jet stream at nearly 700 miles an hour, Thorsness felt as if he had hit a brick wall at full speed. The force of the wind caught his helmet and ripped it off, and thrust his legs sideways at 90 degree angles, tearing up his knees. The parachute opened with such a violent jerk that several panels were shredded.

As he floated down, he saw Johnson in his chute about a mile and a half away. Thorsness pulled out the emergency radio attached to the parachute harness and talked to other pilots flying in the area. "This is Major Leo Thorsness. Get me out of here!" But in his heart, he knew the chances of rescue were slim to none.

During his five-minute descent, he thought about his family. *If I'm killed or captured, will Gaylee and Dawn ever find out?* he wondered. *They could be left in limbo for years.*

He also felt guilty for whatever fate was in store for him and his buddy Harry Johnson. *It's my fault we're in this position. Somehow I made a mistake.* Even though he had shot down two MiGs, destroyed more SAM sites than anyone, and designed new tactics that other pilots were using, all he could think about was, *I made a fatal mistake.*

When he was about 2,000 feet from the ground, he saw little bursts of light coming from the shadows of the mountain forest. *Those are muzzle flashes! They're shooting at me!* He figured he would be captured or killed within the hour because he knew he couldn't walk on his injured knees. But then he heard a voice in his head — a voice he believed was God's — saying over and over, "Leo, you're going to make it . . . Leo, you're going to make it."

He landed in a tall tree and lowered himself to the ground. Unable to walk, he started crawling away, but was quickly captured by a dozen North Vietnamese teenagers brandishing machetes. They cut off his clothes and carried him down the mountain to a large hut on stilts.

Inside the hut, which was lit by torches, tribal men were squatting along the walls and smoking pipes. Johnson was already there, spread-eagled on his back on the floor with his wrists and ankles tied. Thorsness was put in the same position next to him. Whenever one would speak to the other, they were beaten.

The tribesmen chattered among themselves, occasionally pointing at the Americans. Not able to understand Vietnamese, Thorsness whispered to Johnson, "Harry, I think this is a trial, and we're going to be executed."

"Leo, either they will or they won't. We can't control it, so there's no sense worrying about it."

Although his words brought Thorsness a slight peace of mind, they also brought another beating for both of them.

The next night, they were taken to Hanoi's infamous Hoa Lo Prison — called derisively by the POWs the "Hanoi Hilton." Separated from Johnson, Thorsness was dragged to an interrogation room that had knobby concrete walls. He soon learned that it hurt a lot more when you are knocked against knobby walls than against smooth ones.

He was ordered to sit on a small stool in front of two men who were in chairs behind a plain wooden table. They fired questions at him: What was your target? What is your target tomorrow? What is your squadron? Who is your commanding officer?

According to the Geneva Convention, a prisoner of war is required to give only his name, rank, serial number, and date of birth. Physical and mental torture is forbidden. Shamefully, the enemy ignored the Geneva Convention even though they had signed it, claiming the United States never officially declared war against North Vietnam. When Thorsness answered all the questions the same — "Thorsness, Leo K., Major, AO3025937, February 14, 1932" — he was beaten and thrown against the knobby wall.

For the next 19 days and nights, Thorsness was cruelly tortured in the most painful ways imaginable. The agony became unbearable. To cope with the torture, he made himself hallucinate so his mind could, in a sense, separate from his body and free him from the pain.

In this altered state of consciousness, he "talked" with his wife on the other side of the world. He had long conversations with his father, who had died eight years earlier. In his mind, Thorsness went back in time to the family farm near Walnut Grove, Minnesota, where he began his childhood in the throes of the Great Depression. He relived days of feeding chickens, baling alfalfa, milking cows, spreading manure, shucking corn, and slopping pigs with his brother, sister, and his hardworking parents.

Unable to get information out of Thorsness, his captors used torture in a vicious attempt to make him condemn the war. It would have been a propaganda bonanza for an American military officer like Thorsness to denounce the United States for "fighting a war of aggression against a peace-loving nation." He refused.

Despite days of relentless, inhumane treatment, Thorsness uttered only what the Geneva Convention required. He had been taught how to deal with moments like this: Don't give anything until you can't stand the torture anymore. Then give a simple lie that's easy to remember. If a question is insignificant, give an indirect, unclear answer.

After more than two weeks of nonstop torture, Thorsness broke and finally went beyond only giving name, rank, serial number, and date of birth. He didn't tell his interrogators anything remotely worthwhile and lied whenever he could. But he felt distraught that he had broken, believing he had let his country down. He tried to cry but he was beyond tears.

After enduring days and nights of merciless cruelty, he was thrown into a cramped cell with two other POWs. When Thorsness told them he felt like a failure for breaking, Jim Hiteshew, an Air Force major who had been shot down six weeks earlier, eased his mind, telling him, "Everyone who goes through that type of interrogation had one of two things happen to him: They either broke or died — and some did both."

Thorsness suffered severe back injuries from the torture and couldn't walk for nearly a year. Because of his "uncooperative attitude," he was denied medical attention. For three years, he was kept in solitary confinement or with one or two other POWs in a tiny, windowless cell. Meals were twice a day: a bowl of boiled greens with no seasoning and a small plate of steamed rice — with pebbles and bugs in it. If he or the other POWs were heard talking, the guards would beat them or make them kneel on rough concrete for hours.

Despite the threat of severe punishment if they were caught, the POWs managed to communicate with one another in their cells by lightly tapping a secret code on the wall. Within months, he was able to tap out 15 words a minute.

Eventually, Thorsness and others who were in solitary confinement were moved to bigger cells that held from 15 to 45 POWs. Among the 350 POWs at the Hanoi Hilton — mostly Air Force and Navy pilots — were John McCain (who decades later would become a U.S. senator and presidential candidate) and Wild Weasels Tom Madison and Tom Sterling.

Although life was hard and incredibly boring, it was better than what Thorsness had been living during the first three years. The prisoners were allowed to talk and had limited space to walk in the cells. Most days, they were let out for a few minutes to pour a bucket of water over themselves for a bath.

The happiest day for him came toward the end of the third year when he received a letter from his wife, Gaylee.

It was only six lines — which was all the enemy would allow family members to write — but it said so much. She wrote that she had learned he was alive and in prison about a year after he was shot down. Reading that she knew what happened to him was a huge relief for Thorsness. *She knows I'm not dead.* Over the next three years, the enemy limited the number of letters from Gaylee to less than a dozen.

One day in early March 1973, during his sixth year of captivity, Thorsness and the other POWs were ordered to assemble in the prison courtyard. The camp commander stood on a box and gave a stunning announcement: The war had ended, and the POWs would be going home in four groups 15 days apart. Deep down, the POWs wanted to believe him, but they had had their hopes raised and then dashed before. They didn't trust their captors, so when they returned to their cells, there wasn't any smiling or backslapping.

But it was true; the war had ended for the United States. When it was Thorsness's turn to leave, with the second group, he and the others were given a pair of pants, a shirt, and shoes. But he was seriously ill with a high fever and walked with great difficulty. Put on a bus for the airport, he and his comrades weren't cheering because they were still wary that this was all a ploy. But they began to believe freedom was real when they were dropped off at a hangar and handed over to a United States Air Force colonel. While boarding a waiting C-141 cargo plane, they were greeted by nurses who, to Thorsness, looked like beauty queens because they were the first women he had seen in six years. The POWs remained relatively somber as they settled in their seats, and Thorsness was put on a stretcher. But the second the plane was airborne, the POWs' pent-up emotions exploded in cheers and tears.

After the plane touched down hours later at Clark Air Force Base in the Philippines, the POWs had their first chance to call home to their loved ones. Thorsness had spent the previous six years thinking of the perfect opening line if or when he would ever get the chance to phone Gaylee. His first words to her: "I would have called you sooner but I've been all tied up." He thought it was hilarious. She didn't.

He was soon on his way to Scott Air Force Base near St. Louis, where he would undergo further medical treatment for malaria. As the plane neared the West Coast at night, he was called up to the cockpit. Seeing the glow from the lights of San Francisco in the distance ahead, he choked up with emotion.

The pilot let him give the position report to the FAA Control Center. "San Francisco Center, this is Homecoming Seven," Thorsness radioed.

Before he could say any more, he heard a few bars of the song "Don't Fence Me In" on the radio frequency. "Welcome home!" said the air traffic controller. "We've waited a long time."

"Thank you, San Francisco Center. We are two hundred miles due west."

"Homecoming Seven, be advised you have presidential clearance from your present position direct to St. Louis."

Thorsness smiled and thought, *Life is going to be pretty good from now on.*

Seven months after his return to the United States, Leo Thorsness received the Medal of Honor at the White House for demonstrating "extraordinary heroism, self-sacrifice, and personal bravery" during his 87th mission. The medal had been awarded by Congress during his captivity, but wasn't publicly announced until his release from prison to prevent the North Vietnamese from using it against him. The same was true for Harry Johnson, who was awarded the distinguished Air Force Cross for that mission.

Retiring from the military as a colonel, Thorsness entered the business world and politics, serving as a state senator in Washington for four years. He lives with his wife, Gaylee, in Madison, Alabama, near their daughter, Dawn, and two granddaughters.

Thorsness wrote a book about his days as a Wild Weasel and years of captivity called Surviving Hell: A POW's Journey, *published by Encounter Books.*

THE ULTIMATE SACRIFICE

Army Private First Class Milton Olive III

Private First Class Milton "Skipper" Olive would never know that a lakefront park in Chicago, a junior college, and an elementary school would be named after him. He would never know that what he did on October 22, 1965, would earn him the nation's highest military award. He would never know that his actions that day would change the lives of so many people and leave a lasting legacy of love for his fellow man.

What Olive did know in the final seconds of his young life was that he was about to make the ultimate sacrifice for his battle buddies and for his country.

From the moment he took his first breath on November 7, 1946, people tended to underestimate him. His mother, Clara Lee Olive, died just four hours after giving birth to him, and when Milton developed complications, doctors believed that he wouldn't live more than a day or two. They were wrong.

His father, Milton Burris Olive, Jr., who was affectionately known as Big Milt, named the frail baby Milton III, although the boy didn't actually share his dad's middle name. Big Milt gave him the middle name Lee in honor of Clara Lee.

During his early years, Milton — an only child — was raised mostly by Big Milt's cousin Zylphia Wareagle Spencer and her husband, Jacob Augustus Spencer. Zylphia, known as Big Ma, started calling the baby "Skipper," and the name stuck. Although Skipper was small and slightly built, he was a healthy kid. When he was six years old, his father married Antoinette Mainor, a schoolteacher. While growing up in a middle-class neighborhood on Chicago's South Side, the boy was spoiled by Big Milt, who bought him nice clothes and expensive gifts, such as new bicycles and cameras for his birthday or Christmas. Skipper was always the best-dressed kid on the block.

Big Milt, a supervisor for the city's Department of Human Services, had a side business as a professional photographer and shared his passion for photography with Skipper. Often clad in matching suits, father and son snapped pictures at weddings, social functions, and church picnics. Big Milt was so proud of his boy that he made up business cards that read "Milton Oliver III, Chicago's Only 12-year-old Professional Photographer."

THE ULTIMATE SACRIFICE

If Skipper didn't have a camera in his hands, he had a Bible. A regular churchgoer with deep convictions that developed in early childhood, he enjoyed studying the New Testament. The soft-spoken youth was well liked by everyone he met. In contrast to some of his fellow teenagers in the neighborhood, he didn't smoke, drink, swear, or even think about using drugs. He was conservative and serious, and although he held strong beliefs, he wasn't one who would back them up with his fists.

The African-American teenager went through a difficult period at home, so he moved in with his paternal grandparents, Eva Redmond Olive and Milton Olive, Sr., on their farm near Lexington, Mississippi, and attended school there. But he dropped out of high school in his junior year because he felt he wasn't being challenged academically.

While in Lexington, Skipper was angered that racist state officials there were deliberately making it difficult, if not impossible, for blacks to register to vote. He hadn't experienced such blatant racism in Chicago. Wanting to be a part of the civil rights movement, he joined a Mississippi voter registration campaign.

When his grandmother found out what he was doing, she feared for his life. Nine years earlier, in 1955, another African-American teenager from Chicago, 14-year-old Emmett Till, was murdered while visiting relatives in Money, Mississippi. Because the push for civil rights in the South was being met with hostility and violence during Skipper's stay in Mississippi, his grandmother believed his activism would eventually lead to his murder. She couldn't convince him to quit, so she called his father and told him what Skipper was doing.

Worried that the teenager would be targeted by a blood-thirsty racist group such as the Ku Klux Klan, Big Milt ordered him back to Chicago. Big Milt then gave him three options: return to school, get a job, or join the military. So in the summer of 1964, Skipper enlisted in the Army. He was 17. At the time, combat troops weren't fighting in any war, and few Americans had ever heard of Vietnam.

After completing his basic training at Fort Knox, Kentucky, Olive was assigned to advanced training at the Artillery School at Fort Sill, Oklahoma. But when he learned that he could make an extra $50 a month as a "sky soldier," he reported to the Airborne School at Fort Benning, Georgia, for a chance to qualify. Based on his size — he was five feet six and weighed 140 pounds — most drill sergeants figured he would wash out long before completing the difficult training. They were wrong. He might have been the smallest guy in the unit, but he had grit and was determined to prove he could keep up with his fellow trainees, regardless of how big and strong they were. To the surprise of most everyone — including his pals back in Chicago — Olive became a full-fledged U.S. Army paratrooper.

In May 1965 Olive was deployed to Vietnam, where he was assigned to Company B, 2nd Battalion, 503rd Infantry,

173rd Airborne Brigade — one of the first units to see heavy combat in-country. A few weeks after his arrival, he was wounded in a firefight, earning him a Purple Heart. He didn't tell his father at the time because he didn't want Big Milt to worry.

When he came home on leave to recover from his injury, Olive hardly ever took off his uniform because he was so proud to be a paratrooper. He even wore it while watching television with his family. He told them he was anxious to return to Vietnam and finish the job he was trained to do.

Back in Vietnam, Olive and members of Company B took part in an increasing number of firefights with the Viet Cong. In a battlefield letter to a cousin, Olive wrote, "Just a line to say hello. I'm over here in Never Never Land fighting this hellish war. . . . You said I was crazy for joining up. Well, I've gone you one better. I'm an official U.S. Army Paratrooper. How does that grab you? I've made six jumps already." He admitted things had been "pretty tough," but he joked that he was "Uncle Sam's number one man in Vietnam."

The Vietnam War was the first American conflict since the American Revolution that had no units based solely on the racial makeup of the soldiers. Although black servicemen now served in fully integrated units and were represented in all ranks, Olive still had to deal with racial tension in his unit, the 3rd Platoon. A fellow soldier — an 18-year-old white soldier from Charleston, South Carolina — was constantly harassing him. Finally, Olive had taken enough abuse.

THE ULTIMATE SACRIFICE

Although it went against his nature, he duked it out with the other guy behind a tent, where both drew blood. Olive didn't hear any more racist remarks from him. For the most part, blacks and whites got along in the unit because they had no choice. They needed to depend on one another if they were going to survive.

With his easygoing style and likable personality, Olive found it natural to make friends. His comrades called him "Preacher" because during downtime he would read his well-worn Bible and discuss passages with anyone who would listen. He still didn't smoke, drink, or swear, but he was no longer bothered by those who did.

Olive never had a steady girlfriend, although he did write to a certain young lady back home whom he liked. The problem was he didn't know what to say to her, so one of his battle buddies, John "Hop" Foster, a self-described "street-smart cat" from Pittsburgh, helped him out. Foster would create love letters for Olive, who would copy them in his own handwriting and send them off.

Olive's comrades enjoyed kidding him for being naïve and mild-mannered. But by fall, after five months of firefights, he had been in enough skirmishes and seen enough death to turn into an experienced, tough combat veteran. Displaying a can-do attitude, Olive proved he was a good soldier, carrying out orders to the letter without complaint and gaining the respect of officers and enlisted men in his platoon.

THE ULTIMATE SACRIFICE

On the morning of October 22, 1965, helicopters dropped off the men of Company B — the Bravo Bulls — in an area known as the Iron Triangle near Phu Cuong, about 35 miles north of Saigon. They were on a search-and-destroy mission: find the Viet Cong who were operating in the jungle and kill them. Lieutenant Jimmy Stanford, who had joined the unit three days earlier from the Green Berets, was the platoon leader. He reminded his men to be alert, finger on the trigger. They didn't have to be told; they had been carrying out these bloody missions for so long it had become routine.

Third platoon moved on the right flank of the company through vegetation so thick Olive and his comrades could barely see. The men were hot, tired, and wet. For the past few weeks, there had been no letup in the heat and rain as they tramped through the tangled growth. Suddenly, an enemy sniper fired from somewhere in the dark green, his bullet fatally striking a soldier in the head. It was the opening salvo of a VC ambush, and everyone dived for cover before firing back. Olive was one of the first to get up when the Americans counterattacked and pushed deeper into the jungle.

As the platoon pressed on, it was once again pinned down in a second ambush. But the troops retaliated with a vengeance and assaulted several VC positions, causing the enemy to flee.

Olive and his comrades chased after them until coming to a burned-out patch of the jungle that had been scorched by napalm days earlier. As the troops began moving through the clearing, the VC ambushed them for a third time, shooting from the tree line on three sides. Olive and the others ducked behind any little cover they could find, which was mostly charred tree stumps. The enemy laid down such a heavy barrage of bullets that anyone who dared stick his head up was killed instantly. The noise of battle was deafening and became even louder when the VC began throwing grenades from their spider holes and from hidden positions high in the trees.

Olive was pinned down behind some stumps with four comrades — Lieutenant Stanford, 29; Private Foster, 19; Private Lionel Hubbard, 20; and Platoon Sergeant Vince Yrineo, 36. Their faces were buried in the dirt as bullets whizzed inches over their heads. All around them, grenades were exploding, showering them in mud.

Lying on his stomach between Stanford and Foster, Olive tried to remain calm. There was nothing they could do at the moment except wait out the enemy's initial flurry before striking back. While they were hunkered down, a bullet slammed into Foster's helmet, knocking it off with such force that his forehead was badly cut. Foster turned to Olive and asked, "How bad?"

Olive flashed a grin and replied, "You'll live."

Suddenly, a grenade landed in the two-foot-wide space between Olive and Stanford. The two of them, along with Hubbard, Foster, and Yrineo, were just a couple of seconds away from certain death.

THE ULTIMATE SACRIFICE

"Look out, Lieutenant! Grenade!" Olive shouted, staring at the deadly device that was so close he could see the manufacturer's yellow markings on it.

Few people are ever put in a position when they must make a life-or-death decision in a split second. But Olive was. In the time it takes for a bullet to travel 900 meters, or a toad's tongue to snatch a fly, or a person to hiccup, Olive knew exactly what he was going to do, what he *needed* to do. And he did it in an instant.

Olive reached out, grabbed the grenade, and pulled it right into his chest as if he were hugging it. And then it exploded. Curled around the grenade, Olive's body absorbed the full force of the blast and was thrown high in the air. By the time he struck the ground, landing on his back, Olive was dead.

Not so for his comrades. They were alive. Yes, hot shrapnel from the grenade had ripped into Yrineo's face, arm, and chest; had torn into Hubbard's left foot, nearly severing his toes; and had sliced into Stanford's left arm. But they were alive, given the gift of life because the skinny teenager from Chicago chose to die for them.

His action wasn't impulsive; it was instinctive. Above all, it was a true measure of his character, his faith, and his love for his fellow man. It hadn't mattered to Olive, during this era of racial unrest and inequality back in the States, that Stanford was a white guy he hardly knew, Yrineo was a Mexican-American, and Foster and Hubbard were black. They were comrades in arms. They were human beings.

When Private First Class Milton "Skipper" Olive III chose to make the ultimate sacrifice, he was just 16 days shy of his 19th birthday.

After weathering the brutal ambush, Company B fought back, launching a counterattack that soon routed the VC. Before Yrineo was medevacked to the hospital with Hubbard, a soldier picked up a jagged, twisted piece of metal that had been Olive's dog tag, handed it to the sergeant, and said, "Here, Sarge. You'll know what to do with this."

Helping to carry Olive's body out of the jungle was the soldier from South Carolina who had gotten into a fistfight with him weeks earlier.

More than a dozen men were wounded or killed on the day Olive died. Hubbard spent three weeks in the hospital, while Yrineo was out in five days. Stanford didn't even realize he had been struck by shrapnel until he returned to the base camp and saw that his shirt was soaked with blood.

The Army sent Olive's belongings to his family. The items included an AM/FM radio, a camera, a Bible, and even homemade cookies that Big Ma had sent him. Tucked in the Bible was one of his old business cards, "Milton Olive III, Chicago's Only 12-year-old Professional Photographer." Olive's body was flown back to the U.S., where it was buried in a cemetery behind the West Grove Missionary Baptist Church in Lexington, Mississippi.

Six months later, on April 21, 1966, President Lyndon Johnson posthumously awarded Olive the Medal of Honor at the White House, making the soldier the first African-American in the Vietnam War to be so honored. Among those attending the ceremony in the Rose Garden were the hero's father and stepmother, other relatives, Chicago Mayor Richard J. Daley, and two of the men Olive saved — Stanford and Foster.

In the presentation, President Johnson said, in part: "Words can never enlarge upon acts of heroism and duty, but this nation will never forget Milton Lee Olive III. . . . He was compelled by an instinct of loyalty which the brave always carry into conflict. In that incredibly brief moment of decision in which he decided to die, he put others first and himself last. I have always believed that to be the hardest, but the highest, decision that any man is ever called upon to make.

"Who can say what words Private Olive might have chosen to explain what he did? Jimmy Stanford and John Foster, two of the men whose lives he saved that day on that lonely trail in that hostile jungle 10,000 miles from here are standing on the White House steps today because this man chose to die. I doubt that even they know what was on his mind as he jumped and fell across that grenade.

"But I think I do know this: On the sacrifices of men who died for their country and their comrades, our freedom has been built. Whatever it is that we call civilization rests upon the merciless and seemingly irrational fact of history that some have died for others to live, and every one of us who enjoys freedom at this moment should be a witness to that fact.

"So Milton Olive died in the service of a country that he loved, and he died that the men who fought at his side might continue to live. For that sacrifice his nation honors him today with its highest possible award."

Earlier in his speech, President Johnson uttered a line that neatly summed up Olive's legacy: "In dying, Private Milton Olive taught those of us who remain how we ought to live."

The four men whose lives were saved because of Olive's unselfish act eventually married, had children, and grandchildren.

Until the day he died in 2011, Vince Yrineo kept Olive's mangled dog tag as a reminder of the hero's sacrifice. "To me, it's something sacred," he told Olive's cousin Chinta Strausberg years ago.

After leaving the Army, Lionel Hubbard worked at an oil refinery in West Texas. In retirement, he told a reporter, "I prayed to God every day I was over there in Vietnam, 'Please let me make it back.' Thanks to God and Milton, I did."

After the war, John Foster bounced around from job to job for ten years before becoming the manager of an executive parking lot in Miami and embracing a strong religious faith. He told the Chicago Tribune in 2002, "I asked myself, 'Why me? Why was my life saved?' I really think my life was spared for a purpose. I'm not going to be Martin Luther King or Malcolm X, but if there's one soul I can save, one person I can help up, then my life was saved for a reason. I think it was so I could help spread the word of God. All I can do with the gift Milton gave me is to try to pass it on."

Foster and Hubbard have since died.

Jimmy Stanford, who lives in Mexico, says he became a changed man. He admitted that he had a racist streak in him before his life was spared by Olive's actions. "I was raised in the Deep South in the 1940s, and there was a lot of racial tension," Stanford recalls. "That's what I grew up with. That's what I knew. I learned that at home, and it was like learning how to put on your clothes. But when a man sacrifices his life for you, you rethink your learning."

After spending more than 23 years in the Army — including two tours of duty in Vietnam — and rising to the rank of captain, Stanford settled down in San Antonio, Texas, working at various times in construction, at a chemical plant, and for an auto dealership.

In 1992, Stanford drove to Lexington, Mississippi, to visit the grave of the young man who had saved his life. Stanford brought a wreath of plastic flowers made up in red, white, and blue and arranged to look like a flag. At the bottom, it said, "I SHALL NEVER FORGET." He laid the wreath by the headstone that featured a photo of Olive posing in combat gear and an engraving of the Medal of Honor. Stanford then *stepped back from the grave, raised his hand, and saluted his fallen comrade.*

Behind him stood some of Olive's relatives, including Big Milt, who had driven down from Chicago to meet Stanford. The two hadn't seen each other since the Medal of Honor ceremony at the White House in 1966. Following the laying of the wreath, everyone sang "Amazing Grace." A year later, Big Milt passed away.

Today, Private First Class Milton Olive III is memorialized in several places. Among them: Olive Park, on the edge of Lake Michigan, just north of Navy Pier in Chicago; Olive-Harvey College, one of the City Colleges of Chicago, which is named after both Olive and fellow Vietnam soldier and Medal of Honor recipient Carmel B. Harvey, another Chicago native; the Milton L. Olive Middle School in Wyandanch, Long Island, New York; and the Olive Terrace community at Fort Gordon, Georgia.

Says Stanford, "What Olive did was the most incredible display of selfless bravery I ever witnessed."

FLYING IN THE FACE OF DANGER
Army Major Patrick Brady

Anything to save a patient.

That was Major Patrick Brady's motto. As a DUSTOFF helicopter pilot, he felt it was his duty to push himself to the limit — and beyond — in any attempt to rescue wounded soldiers day or night, even under the most horrible flying conditions.

DUSTOFF — which came to stand for Dedicated, Unhesitating Service To Our Fighting Forces — was the call sign for U.S. Army Air Ambulance units.

Like the other DUSTOFF pilots, Brady had to fly in jungle-covered mountainous terrain, sometimes in dense fog and fierce thunderstorms; land in mud, mangroves; and mine-fields; stay there in the middle of a firefight, totally exposed to enemy bullets, rockets, and mortars; load the wounded and dead amidst the shooting and shouting of combat chaos; then get everyone out of there alive. And do this 10, 20, 30, or even 40 times a *day*. For Brady, his high was 42.

DUSTOFF was by far the most hazardous of all aviation operations during the Vietnam War. About a third of all crewmembers were either killed or wounded, and their helicopters were three times more likely to get shot down as other choppers.

At the start of his second tour of duty in Vietnam, in late summer 1967, Brady was part of a new DUSTOFF unit, the 54th Medical Detachment, 67th Medical Group, 44th Medical Brigade, based in Chu Lai. It had 40 men, including 12 pilots, and six helicopters. The job of the flight crew was to pick up wounded, injured, and seriously ill American troops, members of the 2nd ARVN Division and other forces, civilians, and even scout dogs and enemy casualties. Their area of operation — from Da Nang to Duc Pho, a distance of 165 kilometers — was considered at the time the most dangerous in Vietnam because of constant combat, difficult terrain, and treacherous weather conditions.

One of the unit's worst days occurred on September 29, 1967, during its first week of operation. Friendlies had been pinned down in a ditch in an open area near Hiep Duc and had suffered several serious casualties. Three attempts by choppers to get in had failed, including a DUSTOFF that was badly damaged after taking multiple rounds that ruptured a fuel line and shattered the windshield.

FLYING IN THE FACE OF DANGER

Brady and his crew hopped into their Huey — a UH1-H ambulance helicopter — and flew toward the pickup zone (PZ) in another attempt to rescue the wounded. As the crew hovered over ten-foot-tall elephant grass, looking for the casualties, the chopper was struck eight times by bullets, knocking out the fuel gauge and other instruments. Fearing the aircraft was unsafe to fly, Brady landed near the PZ. He discovered that two rounds had struck the tail rotor, making it unfit to fly. So, while soldiers formed a protective shield around Brady and his men, another helicopter came in and brought them back to their base. But their day was just starting. "We need to find another aircraft and get back to work," Brady announced.

Flying his second Huey of the day, Brady headed to an area where a previous DUSTOFF had been riddled with 50 rounds and had barely made it back. Brady's mission was to pick up 11 wounded Americans in deep jungle terrain surrounded by tall trees. As he started to set the helicopter down at what he was told was a secure PZ, two VC jumped out of their spider holes on each side of the aircraft and shot medic Steve Hook and crew chief Henry Hyde through its open doors.

Seeing Hyde slumped over in his harness, Brady thought, *Oh, my God, he's dead!* Brady noticed that Hook was no longer onboard and assumed the medic had toppled out of the aircraft when he was shot. Trying to save the chopper, Brady scooted it forward low on the ground to the far side of the

PZ while the friendlies killed the two VC. By now, a full-blown firefight had erupted, pinning down the soldiers.

Unexpectedly, in the midst of the fury, Brady spotted Hook on the ground. The medic was tromping through the tall grass, dragging a wounded soldier to the helicopter. Relieved that Hook was alive, Brady noticed that blood was seeping through the back of the medic's shirt. Hook ignored the bleeding and repeatedly crossed the battlefield until all 11 casualties were loaded into the Huey. Then the medic gave Brady the thumbs-up. Because there were tall trees on either side of him, Brady had to be extra careful, so he took the chopper straight up, but slowly. *We're going to be an easy target until we clear the trees and get some airspeed,* he thought. Sure enough, the Huey was hit with several rounds, but they failed to cause any major damage.

As the aircraft left the area, Hook discovered Hyde was still alive. Realizing that a bullet had severed an artery in Hyde's leg, Hook quickly applied a tourniquet to stem the bleeding.

Nearly slipping into unconsciousness, Hyde muttered, "Am I going to die?"

"Yes, you are," Hook replied. "But not today." The medic then turned his attention to the rest of the wounded.

"Hook!" Brady shouted from the cockpit. "Stop and take care of your own wounds first!"

But Hook couldn't hear him because his intercom wasn't connected. *He's going to bleed out!* Brady thought. *I have to do something.* Brady had to remain in the pilot's seat and fly the aircraft, because his copilot was dysfunctional from getting shot at for the first time. While flying with one hand, Brady turned around and, with his other hand, grabbed the closest wounded soldier. Because it was too noisy to hear anything other than through earphones, Brady pointed to Hook's bloody back and then to the soldier's first-aid packet. The soldier got the message. He pulled out a bandage and stuck it on Hook's bullet wound while the gutsy medic continued to treat the casualties.

Brady got the wounded safely to the hospital, where Hook and Hyde were treated with the other casualties.

Gathering a new crew, Brady went out again and had several rounds slam into his Huey as he was landing in a hot PZ. One bullet tore open the electrical compartment and another came up under copilot Greg Schwartz's seat, destroying his map and weapon, but missing him — barely. After putting the helicopter on the ground and checking out the damage, Brady determined the chopper was still flyable. So, after the patients were loaded up, he lifted off and brought them safely to the hospital.

Brady's aircraft had been hit with enemy rounds on three different missions in the same day — a day when six helicopters in the unit were shot up.

At the end of the unit's first week, DUSTOFF had evacuated 206 patients and six dead in 109 missions. But nine choppers (including three loaned from other units) had been shot up and five crewmen had been wounded. *We have to do a better job*, Brady thought. And they did. Working 12-hour shifts seven days a week, the DUSTOFF crews continued to improve, saving the lives of an increasing number of wounded.

Despite the obvious danger of his job, Brady didn't worry much about getting shot or getting his Huey blown up by an RPG. No, his greatest fear was failure; that he wouldn't be able to rescue the wounded. It was a fear that drove him to succeed.

Part of his resolve to always do well came from self-reliance, which was honed during an unsettled childhood. Born in South Dakota, he grew up in a broken family, shuttling from place to place and attending 10 schools by the time he entered high school. He also gained strength from his strong Catholic faith, attending Mass daily whenever possible while in Vietnam.

Faith, self-reliance, and fear of failure made him excel as a pilot — especially on January 6, 1968.

Brady was awakened about 7 A.M. and told that two ARVN soldiers were in serious condition at an isolated outpost deep in enemy-held mountainous terrain about 15 minutes southwest of Chu Lai. The outpost, fittingly named Lonely Boy, not only was under attack but it was shrouded in about 400 meters of thick valley fog. Other pilots had made seven attempts to reach the wounded pair but backed off because they felt it was too dangerous to fly blindly in that kind of weather.

Now it was up to Brady. Having developed a new technique for flying in dense fog, he was the go-to guy in zero-visibility conditions.

Even though it was his day off, he summoned a crew, grabbed a reconnaissance map, and headed out on a life-saving mission, just as he had done countless times before. Flying in clear skies at an altitude of 2,000 feet, Brady radioed Lonely Boy and was told that the PZ was being mortared and the troops were under fire. "I'll be there in a few minutes," Brady said. "You won't see me in the fog down there, so listen for my chopper."

Brady's Huey soon hovered above the top of the fog bank that covered Lonely Boy below. Finding a trail on the side of a mountain that matched the one on his map, he slowly started down into the pea soup, guiding his helicopter sideways (perpendicular to the mountain). He looked out his side window during the descent, keeping his eyes locked on two reference points — the tips of his rotor blades and the tops of the trees. He had to stay as close as possible to the mountain so he could see the trail through the fog. If he lost sight of either, he risked crashing.

Even though he faced unchallenged, close-range enemy fire, he landed safely in a confined area a short distance from the designated PZ. After the two patients were loaded onboard, Brady did an instrument takeoff, going straight up through the fog and into the clear, where it was then easy flying to the hospital.

Minutes later, he heard chatter on the radio about 70 casualties at another area that had been savagely attacked by mortars and RPGs for three days. Surrounded by the enemy in a valley below the mountaintop command post called LZ West, many of the wounded had been lying in the mud all night.

"Why aren't they being evacuated?" Brady radioed.

"The fog is too thick, and enemy action is still too hot," came the reply. "There've been rescue attempts, but no one can get in there. Two ships [helicopters] were shot down, and a crew is missing."

Upset that the wounded were not being rescued, Brady loaded a medical team led by Captain Mike Scottie, a respected field physician, and flew toward the besieged outpost. Brady requested the radio frequency and location of the casualties, but the brigade commander, a colonel in charge of LZ West, refused, explaining, "It's too dangerous. I don't want to risk losing another crew or another chopper."

Frustrated, Brady landed at LZ West. As diplomatically as a major can be with a higher-ranking colonel, Brady told him, "We can get those guys out, and we should do it right now. There's no need for them to suffer and die without us trying. I know how to get in there in the fog. We just made a successful pickup 20 klicks [kilometers] away in identical circumstances."

"It's impossible in this situation," the commander claimed.

Brady was beside himself. He had never before been denied the chance to at least try to evacuate casualties. He kept pleading his case to whoever would listen: "I can't imagine leaving somebody in the field. In our unit, we never go home without our patients. If a pilot can't get them, he'll call for help. And the next guy goes in and tries. And if he fails, another one will try, and so on until all the patients are rescued. No, the 54th will never leave anybody in the field."

Meanwhile, the colonel radioed a medic on the battlefield near the base of the mountain. The medic verified that many of the wounded were in serious condition and would die unless they were evacuated immediately. The enemy was now only 50 meters away from them. Softening his position, the colonel turned to Brady's copilot and asked, "Can you guys really make it in there?"

"Absolutely," the copilot declared. "We've done it many times before in this kind of weather. We did it this morning."

The colonel then talked it over with Brady. "I want you to know what you're in for," the colonel said. "The friendlies are surrounded, and the enemy has sixteen 12.7-mm anti-aircraft guns that shot down the other birds [choppers]. One of the crews is still missing. If I give you the frequency and location, you're on your own. I won't lift the artillery."

The night before, the colonel had temporarily stopped an artillery barrage on the enemy position so other helicopters would have a safer time in the rescue attempt of the downed chopper crew. Unfortunately, the effort had failed, and the enemy had been given a breather from the bombardment.

"Your artillery has nothing to do with my mission," Brady said. "The chances of us getting hit from your artillery are slimmer than a flying bird getting hit from a thrown rock. It's not going to happen. Colonel, please let me do my job to rescue those men. They're suffering needlessly right below us only a few minutes away."

The colonel relented and gave Brady the frequency and location of the beleaguered unit, which had the call sign Twister Charlie. Because of the number of casualties, the colonel asked Brady to take four other helicopters with him. After explaining to the pilots his technique for dropping into a fog bank, he took off and had the other choppers follow him in a line. But once they were airborne, he lost radio contact with them and was relieved when they turned back. *It'd be a mess in the fog with five birds and no inter-aircraft commo,* he thought.

Brady carefully hovered down the mountain away from LZ West and into the fog, keeping his eye on a road until he neared the valley floor. Flying at only ten feet above the ground, he guided his Huey toward the patients' position.

To his surprise, he flew a few feet directly over a uniformed NVA unit, but disappeared into the fog before they could react and start shooting. *They were probably as startled as I was,* he thought.

The enemy tried to lure him back by popping yellow smoke in the mist, hoping he would think the signal came from friendlies. But he was in radio contact with Twister Charlie and knew it was a trap. With guidance from the troops, Brady landed at the right spot, dropped Captain Scottie off, and loaded up more than a dozen wounded. Although their comrades were still engaged in a brutal firefight, Brady wasn't too worried that his aircraft would get hit. *There's no way anyone can see anything in this stuff,* he thought. *We're safe.* Relying solely on his instruments, he lifted his chopper straight up through the fog.

Some of the LZ West troops on top of the mountain burst into cheers when they looked down and saw the Huey emerge from the valley fog below. After Brady landed, the impressed medical officer saluted him, even though the officer outranked him.

The patients were offloaded and put in other choppers for transportation to the hospital. Meanwhile, Brady went back. Again, the same four helicopters tried to follow him, and again they turned around, leaving him to carry on the mission solo.

Concerned that the enemy might be waiting for him this time, Brady took a slightly different course, using a stream that snaked down the mountain as his guide during his descent into the fog. Within an hour, he and his crew made four trips to the embattled landing zone and brought all 70 casualties out safely. Twister Charlie was so beat up that the unit was declared combat ineffective and removed from the battlefield.

A few minutes after leaving LZ West, Brady, whose call sign was DUSTOFF 55, received word from a unit known as Savage Golf that two wounded troops were in urgent need of evacuation. The unit was under attack, and the voice on the radio sounded stressed and confused.

Savage Golf was desperate to get the casualties out and told Brady the PZ — located in a confined area surrounded by jungle and rice paddies — was secure. Brady had his doubts. *Those guys would lie to get a wounded buddy out; in truth, so would I.* "Savage Golf, this is 55," he radioed. "I see purple smoke. Is that you?" After receiving assurance it was, Brady replied, "Roger, we are coming down."

As his Huey settled over the elephant grass near the smoke signal, Brady didn't see anyone — no friendlies, no patients. "Where are they?" he asked his crew.

The medic stuck his head out the open door and reported, "They're prone in the grass directly below us. But no one is standing up. No one is moving."

Brady hated moments like this when his helicopter was just hovering all alone, because it was now an easy target for the enemy. He could feel his veins bulge and his heart pound. His muscles tensed up and his ears burned from the tension.

The troops were pinned down by the enemy, which suddenly took aim at the Huey. Brady's aircraft shuddered as bullets struck under the cockpit and near the flight controls. Before sustaining any more damage to the chopper, Brady flew up and out of the fog. Above the fray, he examined and tested the flight controls, and figured the aircraft was still flyable.

The radio operator for Savage Golf begged Brady to come back for another attempt.

"Savage Golf, this is 55," Brady radioed in response. "We are still overhead. We took several rounds while we were sitting down in that area. What is your situation right now?"

"The PZ is secure."

Yeah, that's what he said before, Brady thought. *I'll give it one more shot.* "Savage Golf, if I come in again, are you going to have those patients ready for me? Are you guys going to stand up and help load them?"

"Affirmative. They'll be in the same area you landed before."

Then an officer for Dragon Six, a command unit, came on the air sounding a bit too incredulous for Brady's confidence: "DUSTOFF, are you really going in there *again*?"

"Affirmative," Brady replied. Contacting Savage Golf, Brady radioed, "This is 55. We will be coming in the same way we did the last time. Hold your fire until we get in there. If we hear any fire, we're going to have to abort because we won't be able to tell who is shooting."

Savage Golf responded, "Smoke will expose our position. Can you find us without it?"

"Negative, pop smoke because I don't know exactly where you are." As he descended, Brady said, "Keep talking to me now. Am I coming toward you?"

"Yes, I hear you!"

This time when Brady landed, the troops got up out of the grass and hurriedly loaded the patients while under fire. Through the flying bullets, Brady got his crippled Huey up and out of danger and coaxed it back to the base in Chu Lai where the wounded were offloaded.

After Brady's chopper was examined, the maintenance chief told him, "You're lucky to bring this bird back in one piece. Your controls were severely damaged, and there's only a paper-thin amount of metal between the controls and no controls at all."

Brady obtained a replacement helicopter and immediately flew toward another unit that had reported several casualties. As he neared the location, he was warned that the PZ was hot.

Each mission presented a new challenge and a new learning experience because Brady, like all DUSTOFF pilots, flew by the seat of his pants. To help him determine the safest approach for this particular hot PZ, he tried to picture in his mind what he would see from the enemy's point of view. Fog was not an issue. Once he learned the location of the enemy, he was able to slip in relatively undetected and pick up 12 casualties.

Later, while monitoring radio traffic, Brady heard of troops trapped in a minefield. Six were dead and the rest were wounded, including the commander. The injuries were so serious — loss of limbs, and severe head and body wounds — that the casualties needed immediate evacuation.

As he flew over the area, he saw a DUSTOFF from a sister unit on the ground waiting for the patients. Before that chopper could get loaded, a mine detonated near the aircraft, killing two more soldiers. Believing it was too dangerous to stay a second longer, the other pilot left without picking up any of the wounded.

We can't leave those grunts to die, Brady thought. He radioed the other pilot, "I'm going in."

"Be advised that the mines are command detonated [activated by the enemy], and the company is under fire," the other pilot warned.

"I'm still going in," Brady declared. He knew there was a risk that the downdraft from his rotor blades could set off a mine. But he had seen where the other pilot had landed, so

Brady felt confident that if he could set down in the exact same location, he wouldn't trigger another blast. The spot had good protection, so he wasn't too worried about enemy fire. As carefully as he could, Brady gently landed right on the money, putting his skids exactly where the other chopper had been sitting.

No one from the unit on the ground moved toward the Huey because they were dead, too injured, or too scared to run across the lethal minefield. Brady turned around and saw the uneasy look in the eyes of veteran crewmembers Jim "Pappy" Coleman and Ron "Frenchie" Tweed. "Well," Brady said, "go get 'em."

Coleman and Tweed bravely hustled through the minefield and began carrying patients and the dead back to the helicopter. Trying to follow the exact same path that they had taken the first time, they made several trips. Brady thought, *Things are going well.*

The two crewmen were carrying the large body of an apparently dead soldier on a stretcher and were nearing the chopper when another mine exploded right underneath them. The explosion pitched Coleman and Tweed so high in the air that the horrified Brady feared they might hit the rotors. Shrapnel ripped into the side of the aircraft as well as into the crewmen who landed hard on the ground.

Oh, no! Not Pappy and Frenchie!

To his amazement, both men were not seriously injured and staggered to their feet. Coleman's uniform was smoldering, but he patted out the fire. Although Coleman and Tweed were hurt, they finished loading the patients. After everyone was on board, copilot Pete Schuster examined the aircraft for damage while Brady checked out his crewmen. *The only possible reason Coleman and Tweed survived is that the soldier on the litter took most of the blast,* Brady thought. The chopper was badly peppered, too.

To Brady, Coleman epitomized the DUSTOFF medic: completely fearless, incredibly competent, and dedicated to saving lives. Brady admired the way the medic laughed off peril. During a mission months earlier, Coleman had been helping the wounded to the chopper in an extremely hot PZ when a bullet had passed across his face, slicing open his lips. When a fellow soldier had rushed to his aid, Coleman had quipped through the blood, "I'm good to go. I just kissed the bullet that had my name on it."

Now, after checking over the Huey for damage from the mine blast, Schuster announced that it was flyable. They took off with their patients and headed for the hospital — but at a low altitude just in case a critical part stopped working. Fortunately, the damaged aircraft made it back safely. When Brady looked over the helicopter, he was amazed to see hundreds of shrapnel holes in it.

FLYING IN THE FACE OF DANGER

He then got in his third chopper of the day, and continued a string of lifesaving missions that went on late into the night. By the time the weary Brady had plopped in bed, he and his crew had rescued more than 100 wounded soldiers for the day. *Yep,* he thought before closing his eyes, *anything to save a patient.*

During his two tours in Vietnam, Patrick Brady flew more than 2,500 combat missions and evacuated more than 5,000 wounded.

For his perseverance in the face of extraordinary peril during his lifesaving missions of January 6, 1968, Brady was awarded the Medal of Honor at the White House on October 9, 1969. He continued to serve in the U.S. Army and rose to the rank of major general before retiring in 1993 after 34 years of service.

Brady, who earned a master's degree in business administration at Notre Dame University, served on the boards of several patriotic organizations and is a former president of the Congressional Medal of Honor Society. He takes part in the group's character development program by speaking to students on the importance of courage, sacrifice, and patriotism. Brady wrote about his days as a U.S. Army air ambulance pilot in his book, Dead Men Flying: Victory in Viet Nam, *published by World Net Daily.*

Brady and his wife, Nancy, who live in San Antonio,

Texas, have three sons and three daughters. They all were in the military, including two sons who attended West Point and a daughter who served in Iraq.

Brady's crewmen, Ron Tweed and Jim Coleman, were awarded the Silver Star for courageously running out into the minefield to rescue the wounded.

THE SOLDIER WHO REFUSED TO DIE

Army Staff Sergeant
Roy P. Benavidez

Deep in the jungles of Vietnam near the Cambodian border, Sergeant Roy P. Benavidez crept along a narrow trail on a secret mission to gather evidence that well-trained NVA soldiers were posing as Viet Cong. He himself looked like a VC, carrying a Russian-made AK-47 and wearing black pajamas, sandals fashioned from tire treads, and a cone-shaped straw hat.

It was January 1966 — the beginning of the buildup of American combat troops. The 11-year Army veteran had been in-country since October, acting as an adviser to a South Vietnamese infantry unit. But he also carried out classified operations like the one he was doing today, alone and in peasant garb.

He was walking in stealth mode, quietly and carefully. His eyes darted left and right, looking for any telltale signs of the enemy, while he listened for any unusual sounds.

Then . . . *KA-BOOM!*

Sometime later, a squad of Marines came upon what they assumed was the body of a dead VC who had stepped on a land mine. Wary that the body was booby-trapped, they carefully flipped him over and were surprised to see he was Hispanic, not Asian. When they searched him, they found a set of U.S. Army dog tags sewn into the label of his black pajamas: BENAVIDEZ, SGT R P.

A corpsman kneeled down, felt for a pulse, and shouted, "He's alive!"

Benavidez had stepped on a land mine, but, miraculously, it hadn't blown him to pieces. When it had gone off, a giant piece of metal had flown out of the ground and struck him square in the rear end, twisting his spine like a corkscrew, shattering bone and cartilage in his legs and back, and traumatizing his brain.

Eventually transported to Brooke Army Medical Center (BAMC) in Fort Sam Houston, San Antonio, Texas, Benavidez was paralyzed from the waist down. He suffered amnesia and was unresponsive to those around him for more than two months. When he eventually regained his senses and was able to talk, he had virtually no memory of what had happened to him.

The doctors told him in no uncertain terms that even

though his spinal cord was intact, his injuries were so severe he would never walk again. But Benavidez refused to believe them. He had come too far and had worked too hard to be cast out of the Army and left as a wheelchair-bound civilian. He knew — he absolutely *knew* — they were wrong.

They had no clue how perseverance and tenacity were riveted in his soul. They had no idea how his extraordinarily tough and heartbreaking childhood fueled his drive and ambition. And they had no hint that this broken man, this paraplegic with an attitude, would eventually return to active duty and one day carry out an act of heroism so astounding that it earned him the military's most prestigious combat award.

Benavidez had a never-give-up, never-give-in mentality almost from the day he was born near Cuero, Texas, in 1935 to parents of Mexican and Yaqui Indian descent. When Benavidez, whose given name was Raul, was two years old, his father died of tuberculosis. His mother, who worked as a cleaning lady, remarried but died of the same disease when the boy was seven. He and his younger brother, Rogelio, then moved in with their grandfather, uncle, aunt, and eight cousins in El Campo, Texas.

Throughout his childhood, Benavidez proved to be a hard worker and an even tougher fighter. Sparked by a flash temper, he ended arguments with kids on the street with his fists and refused to back down from anyone. He battled racism daily, enduring taunts of "dumb Mexican," and being turned away from restaurants that displayed signs declaring, "No Mexicans or Dogs. Colored Around Back." To help support the family, he shined shoes at the local bus station and joined relatives doing backbreaking labor as a migrant worker, picking beets in Colorado and cotton in Texas.

At age 15, Benavidez dropped out of high school and worked at a tire store. Eventually he realized that he had no future and no direction, so in 1955, the five-foot, six-inch, 130-pound 19-year-old enlisted in the Army. When his drill sergeant kept mocking him by yelling "Ra-oooool!" the annoyed Benavidez changed his name to Roy. The recruit still had a temper that often got him in trouble, but he adapted to the military way of life and decided to make it his career.

By 1959, he was married and a member of the 82nd Airborne, one of the most elite forces in the military, and traveled the world as an adviser and trainer. In October 1965 he was deployed to Vietnam at a time when Americans served only as advisers to the South Vietnamese. Back then, there were few U.S. casualties. Benavidez, who also conducted covert operations, happened to be one of the unlucky ones when he had stepped on the land mine during his secret mission.

When he awakened in the hospital in Vietnam, he stared at a priest, who was giving him last rites. Unable to fully form words because of his brain injury, Benavidez yelled in his face, making it clear that this soldier wasn't ready to die.

Two months later, at BAMC, he rejected the doctors' prognosis that he would remain a paraplegic and never walk again. Comforted by a strong Catholic faith, Benavidez believed that he had been spared for some greater purpose other than to sit in a wheelchair for the rest of his life. He begged and battled the staff not to discharge him from the military. The Army was his home, his job, his future. He demanded that they give him time to regain the use of his legs . . . and then he set out to do just that.

The first night of his self-imposed therapy, he used his arms to roll out of bed and fall to the floor with a painful thud. The nurse and orderlies chewed him out and put him back in his bed. The next night, he deliberately fell to the floor and dragged himself to the nearest wall. The third night, he put two hands on top of adjoining nightstands and pulled himself up. When he tried to put weight on his legs, he felt a stabbing pain shoot up his back. Despite the excruciating discomfort, Benavidez continued this routine night after night until he could push the nightstands ahead with his arms and drag his body.

And then one night he stood on his own; his weak legs held his weight but tortured him with pain. He pressed on, and after several agonizing weeks, he was able to slowly shuffle. Each night, he hobbled a longer distance than previously until disbelieving doctors, nurses, and therapists realized that, yes, this hardheaded, no-quit-in-him soldier could regain use of his legs — just like he said he would.

THE SOLDIER WHO REFUSED TO DIE

In July, six months after he had arrived at BAMC, Roy Benavidez walked out of the hospital. He needed to hold his wife, Lala's, hand for support, and he remained in terrible pain (which he hid from the doctors), but he *walked*. And he was still in the Army, having been declared fit for limited duty, which for him meant a desk job at Fort Bragg, North Carolina.

He hated it because he wanted to be a soldier again. So he kept pushing himself physically by walking longer, then jogging faster, then running harder. A dream began to form. He wanted to become a member of the elite of the elite — Special Forces, the famed Green Berets. After doctoring some transfer papers, Benavidez got his chance to qualify in a brutal training regimen that washed out 70 percent of the candidates. Like the others, he ran five miles a day carrying a 70-pound backpack, tackled obstacle courses, made parachute jumps, and was left alone in the wilderness for 12 days with barely any food and water. His determination was strong and so was his back pain. But he persevered, and soon his dream came true. He became a Green Beret.

In January 1968 the 33-year-old staff sergeant was deployed for his second tour to Vietnam, where now nearly a half million American troops were fighting and 16,000 of their brothers had already been killed in action. He was assigned to the 5th Special Forces Group's B-56, a unit devoted to gathering intelligence about the NVA.

THE SOLDIER WHO REFUSED TO DIE

About 1:30 P.M. on May 2 at a Green Beret outpost in Loc Ninh, Benavidez was attending a small prayer service held by a chaplain who was using the hood of a Jeep as the altar. The service was interrupted by the sound of automatic weapons fire coming over the radio in a nearby tent and a voice begging, "Get us out of here! For God's sake, get us out!"

Hours earlier, a Special Forces team of three Americans and nine Vietnamese, led by one of Benavidez's best friends, Sergeant First Class Leroy Wright, had been secretly dropped by helicopter into enemy-occupied territory across the Cambodian border to gather intelligence. Now they were being attacked from all sides by an entire NVA battalion. Several attempts had been made to extract the team without success; one chopper was shot down, and two others were riddled with bullets.

The two badly damaged aircraft made it back to Loc Ninh, but without any members of the Special Forces team. Benavidez raced up to the second helicopter, where 19-year-old crew chief Michael Craig, who had been shot several times, was slumped forward in his harness. After getting him on the ground, Benavidez called for help and held him in his arms as the gasping soldier uttered his final words, "Oh, my God, my mother and father . . ."

After making some hasty repairs, pilot Larry McKibben and his crew volunteered to make another rescue attempt. As the engine started up, Benavidez hopped aboard. He didn't wait for orders or permission from anyone to go.

Those were his brothers out there in mortal danger, and he had to do something, even if he had acted so impulsively that he forgot his M16 and had a Special Forces knife as his only weapon.

When the chopper flew over the area, Benavidez saw that the team below had formed a small circle near the pickup zone, but a large number of enemy soldiers were closing in and firing at them, some from only 25 meters away. The helicopter dropped low, ran into withering enemy fire, and backed away.

"I can't get down there," McKibben said. "It's too hot."

"Just get me as close as you can," Benavidez replied.

While other gunships tried to draw fire away from the chopper, McKibben's helicopter zigzagged through a curtain of bullets to another clearing about 75 meters away where it hovered three meters off the ground. After making the sign of the cross, Benavidez threw a medical bag out the door and jumped. He landed on his feet, picked up the bag, and started running. Seconds later, an AK-47 bullet ripped into his right leg, and he crumpled to the ground. But he bounced right up and kept moving.

Just before reaching the tree line, he was blown off balance from the blast of a nearby grenade that sent shrapnel tearing into his arms, forehead, and face, missing his eyes by a fraction of an inch. Undeterred by the pain and the blood running down his face, he got up and headed over to the men who were lying in a brush pile. Four of them, including his buddy Leroy Wright, were dead. The other eight, who were in two separate groups, were badly injured, some beyond the ability to fight back. One of the wounded was his friend, Staff Sergeant Lloyd "Frenchie" Mousseau, who had just lost his right eye from an enemy bullet but was still firing his weapon.

Benavidez bound their wounds and injected morphine to dull their pain. Ignoring NVA bullets and grenades, he passed around ammunition that he had stripped from several bodies and armed himself with an AK-47 from a dead NVA soldier.

Using Mousseau's radio, Benavidez called McKibben and said, "You better come get us fast. We're in real bad shape."

About 20 meters away, Specialist 4th Class Brian O'Connor, the radioman, was moaning, having been shot in the arm, leg, ankle, and stomach. He and a seriously wounded Vietnamese interpreter were lying on the ground.

"We're going to live!" Benavidez shouted to them. "We don't have permission to die yet. Not here."

Just then Benavidez took another round in the thigh. Wincing in pain, he repositioned the men for better covering fire. Then he sent green smoke to signal McKibben to come in. As the helicopter hovered a few meters over the PZ, Benavidez yelled for everyone to run to the chopper. Those who could move under their own power made it to the aircraft while Benavidez hefted and lugged the wounded and the dead one at a time. A soldier who had been shot in the face and had a bandage over his eyes held on to Benavidez's neck. Another comrade, who had been shot in both legs, was dragged to the helicopter.

But O'Connor and the interpreter didn't budge. The chopper lifted a few meters off the ground and moved toward them. Running beneath the helicopter, Benavidez fired the enemy rifle he had picked up until he neared the two men. With his encouragement, the pair began crawling toward the chopper while he went over to Wright's body. There was no way Benavidez would leave his pal behind. Besides, Wright was carrying classified documents, call signs, radio codes, and maps that needed to be kept out of enemy hands. While Benavidez was stuffing the papers under his shirt, shrapnel from a grenade tore into his stomach. Then he took a third bullet, this time in the back. He pitched forward, face down in the ground, and briefly lost consciousness.

When he woke up, he was soaked in blood and gasping for breath. His misery grew worse when he saw the chopper was on its side and in smoking ruins. He didn't learn until later that as the helicopter was hovering a few feet over the PZ, McKibben was fatally shot and lost control, causing the aircraft to tip over and crash. A door gunner was also killed, but everyone else managed to get out. The survivors, including Mousseau, were huddled by the tail section, returning fire. O'Connor and the interpreter were lying nearby, still alive.

Struggling to his feet and holding his stomach, Benavidez gathered the men and led them to a safer place in a small clump of trees where he set up a perimeter. He gave the most seriously wounded morphine shots and injected the drug in himself, too. Under increasing enemy automatic-weapons and grenade fire, he moved around the perimeter distributing water and ammo to his weary men, urging them to keep fighting despite their physical agony and mental anguish, which he was also suffering from.

The enemy — an estimated 350 NVA soldiers — was firing at them from everywhere. Wood and vegetation flew in all directions from the flurry of bullets and mortar rounds. Some of the wounded were hit again, including Benavidez, who took another round in the leg.

"Are you hit bad, Sarge?" one of the men asked him.

"No," Benavidez replied, "I've been hit so many times I don't care anymore."

Facing a buildup of enemy troops that were closing in on the beleaguered team, Benavidez called in tactical air strikes. Within minutes, fighter jets dropped napalm and cluster bombs, momentarily stalling the NVA's advance. Even though he could hardly see because of all the blood streaming down his face, he directed the fire from supporting gunships as he waited for another helicopter to land.

Soon, a chopper piloted by Warrant Officer Roger Waggie and manned by a volunteer crew landed about 30 meters away from the group. "It's now or never!" Benavidez told the wounded men, yelling at them to run to the helicopter.

Limping badly from all his bullet and shrapnel wounds, a grimacing Benavidez helped carry and drag some of his wounded and dead comrades. The NVA were now firing directly at the chopper. Waggie and his copilot were shooting back with their pistols through their blown-out front windshield while the door gunners were firing M60 machine guns at separate groups of NVA charging from the sides.

Two wounded team members were shot in the back as they boarded the aircraft. Despite being barely able to see because blood was dripping in his eyes, Benavidez found Mousseau, who was lying nearly unconscious in the grass.

As Benavidez reached down to pick him up, an NVA soldier rushed up behind him. The soldier slammed his rifle butt into the back of Benavidez's head. Stunned, Benavidez wheeled around and was clubbed again, this time across the face. He fell to the ground. But he refused to stay down, refused to be killed like this. He had been fighting nonstop for six grueling hours and had gone through too much combat to give up now. Reeling in pain, he still had enough sense to pull out the lone weapon he had — his Special Forces knife. As Benavidez started to get up, the NVA soldier lunged forward with his bayonet. Benavidez grabbed it, and even though it slashed his right hand, he yanked the attacker toward him. Then, with his free hand, Benavidez stabbed him in the stomach. Before the foe died, his bayonet severely gored the sergeant's left forearm.

Operating solely on adrenaline and survival instinct, the bloodied, shouting Benavidez directed the men to the chopper. His energy all but tapped out, he assisted two weak comrades and started toward the helicopter. As he drew near, he spotted two NVA soldiers sneaking up toward the aircraft but out of sight of the door gunners. Benavidez picked up a nearby rifle and shot the pair.

With little strength remaining, he made one last trip to the perimeter to make sure everyone was on board and that all classified material had been collected or destroyed. Exhausted and weak from loss of blood, he collapsed in the arms of the helicopter crew who pulled him in. Benavidez was the last American to leave the battlefield.

Even though the helicopter was badly shot up and the instruments weren't working, Waggie managed to get it airborne and out of the area.

On the way back to Loc Ninh, Benavidez, fighting hard to stay conscious, lay on the bloody floor next to Mousseau, who was staring at him with his one good eye. Benavidez held his hand and prayed that they both would live. He felt Mousseau's fingers dig into his palm for several seconds before going totally limp. He knew then his buddy was dead — the team's sixth KIA.

When the helicopter landed, Benavidez had lost so much blood and was so severely wounded that he couldn't talk or move. His jaw was broken, his intestines were exposed, and his body had 37 puncture wounds. He was barely breathing and couldn't open his eyes because they were caked in dried blood. But he could hear, and what he heard frightened him more than any of the horrors he had endured throughout the day. "There's nothing we can do for him," the doctor announced.

Believing he was dead, a medic placed him in a body bag and began closing it up. Inches from being entombed in the bag, Benavidez was frantically trying to find a way to show them he was still alive. So he spit in the medic's face. The medic called over the doctor, who placed his hand on Benavidez's chest and detected a faint heartbeat. "He won't make it," the doctor said, "but we'll try."

If the doctor had understood who his patient was, he might have come up with a different assessment. When Benavidez woke up in a hospital in Saigon, he was happy to see that O'Connor was in a bed across the ward. Neither could move nor speak, so they wiggled their toes every morning to signal each other they were still alive. But then one morning, Benavidez saw that O'Connor's bed was empty and assumed he had died.

Benavidez underwent numerous operations as doctors fought to save his life. He was then transferred to a hospital in Japan for more surgery before he was sent to BAMC for a recovery that took almost a year.

While hospitalized in Texas, he learned that he would receive the Distinguished Service Cross — the second highest combat award for valor. In a bedside ceremony attended by the sergeant's family and friends, General William Westmoreland, the chief of staff of the Army, presented him with the medal.

That night, Benavidez lay in bed and stared at the medal for a long time. He felt proud and sad — proud that the Army honored him for his actions of May 2 and sad that so many brave men had died that day.

The morning after the ceremony, a doctor congratulated Benavidez on his medal, saying, "What you did that day was awesome."

Benavidez shook his head and replied, "No, that was duty."

Although Roy Benavidez's commander believed that the courageous staff sergeant deserved the Medal of Honor, the officer made an official recommendation for the Distinguished Service Cross. The commander knew the process for awarding a Medal of Honor took a long time and he was convinced that Benavidez would die before he got it. Wanting to give Benavidez some recognition for his bravery while the soldier was still alive, the commander was able to get the Distinguished Service Cross rushed through for approval and presentation. Leroy Wright and Lloyd Mousseau were each awarded the medal posthumously. Roger Waggie, the helicopter pilot who got them out, was given the Silver Star.

After he was released from the hospital in May 1969, Benavidez became a master sergeant and remained in the Army for another seven years. In his retirement years, he lived with his wife and three children, Noel, Yvette, and Denise, in El Campo, Texas. He spoke at schools and colleges and even runaway shelters. He encouraged students to stay in school, promoted continuing education, and supported programs that kept young people off drugs.

When his former commander learned that Benavidez had survived the war, the officer gathered more details of the soldier's heroics and recommended him for the Medal of Honor, but the Decorations Board rejected it because there were no American eyewitnesses on the ground during that battle. In 1980, Benavidez's hometown newspaper ran a story critical of the decision. The article was picked up by the press and republished throughout the world, but the publicity didn't sway the board to change its mind. Without an American eyewitness, there would be no Medal of Honor for Benavidez.

Unknown to Benavidez and the Army brass, Brian O'Connor, the radioman in that May 2 firefight, was alive and well and living in the Fiji Islands in the South Pacific. While he had been recovering from his near-fatal wounds in 1968, he had been transferred to a different hospital before officers could fully question him about the battle.

THE SOLDIER WHO REFUSED TO DIE

O'Connor had assumed that Benavidez had died, while Benavidez had assumed O'Connor had died. In one of those amazing twists of fate, O'Connor was on vacation in Australia when, by chance, he read the reprinted story about Benavidez. O'Connor soon phoned his old friend in Texas and then provided the one element that the Army needed to upgrade Benavidez's award — an American eyewitness on the ground.

On February 24, 1981 — almost 13 years after nearly dying to save his comrades — Benavidez received the Medal of Honor at the Pentagon. Minutes before the ceremony, President Ronald Reagan told reporters, "You are going to hear something you would not believe if it were a script. Wait until you hear the citation."

Benavidez didn't regard himself as a hero. "The real heroes are the ones who gave their lives for their country," he told reporters. "I don't like to be called a hero. I just did what I was trained to do."

In 1988, he wrote The Three Wars of Roy Benavidez (published by Pocket Books), which described his struggles growing up as a poor Mexican-American orphan, his military training and combat in Vietnam, and the efforts by others to get recognition for his actions in Vietnam. In 1995, he co-authored with John R. Craig, Medal of Honor: A Vietnam Warrior's Story (published by Brassey's), re-released in 2005 as Medal of Honor: One Man's Journey from Poverty and Prejudice (published by Potomac Books).

THE SOLDIER WHO REFUSED TO DIE

Master Sergeant Roy Benavidez died on November 29, 1998, at age 63 from complications of diabetes. More than 1,500 people attended his funeral. He is buried in the shade of a live oak tree at the Fort Sam Houston National Cemetery.

Among the places that bear his name are: the Master Sergeant Roy P. Benavidez Special Operations Logistics Complex at Fort Bragg, North Carolina; Fort Roy P. Benavidez youth booth camp in Uvalde, Texas; three Roy P. Benavidez Elementary Schools in Texas; and a park in Colorado. A bronze statue of him stands across the street from Cuero (Texas) High School. The U.S. Navy named a cargo ship after him in 2003.

RESCUE AT KHAM DUC

Air Force Lieutenant Colonel Joe Jackson

From the cockpit of his two-engine Air Force cargo plane, Lieutenant Colonel Joe Jackson stared at the carnage below. Two swarming NVA regiments were attacking the besieged U.S. Special Forces camp at Kham Duc with heavy fire from artillery, mortars, and recoilless rifles.

The unrelenting barrage had become so overpowering that Army General William Westmoreland, commander of U.S. forces in South Vietnam, had ordered the camp evacuated. Beginning early in the morning, Army and Marine helicopters and Air Force transport planes had launched a frantic rescue operation under withering fire in a desperate effort to save more than 1,700 American troops and South Vietnamese soldiers and civilians, including women and children.

While Jackson circled overhead at 9,000 feet, hostile forces reached the edge of the burning camp. Their gun placements in the surrounding hills were pounding Kham Duc and its lone runway, while ammunition dumps were exploding and littering the runway with debris. Jackson winced as he surveyed the smoldering wreckage of helicopters and fixed-wing aircraft that had crashed on or next to the airstrip from direct hits during the hectic rescue attempt.

Despite the devastation from the fierce attack, by late afternoon the 1,500 surviving troops and civilians had been evacuated — all except for three American airmen who had been left behind in the chaos.

While still orbiting over the camp, Jackson watched a fellow pilot land a transport plane on the embattled airstrip in a courageous effort to retrieve the men. But in the midst of a thunderous fusillade of automatic weapons and mortars, the pilot was forced to take off before the airmen on the ground could reach the plane.

Realizing that the stranded trio would likely be captured or killed within minutes, Jackson volunteered to try to save them even though he knew there was a strong possibility that he and his crew would be blasted out of the sky. With complete faith in his men, Jackson put his C-123 into a steep dive toward the battered runway. As antiaircraft guns blazed away, he thought, *I know I'm going to get shot. I wonder how badly it will hurt.*

* * *

From as far back as he could remember, Joe Madison Jackson dreamed of becoming a pilot. After seeing a plane do barrel rolls and loops among the clouds when he was five years old, Joe told his dad, "When I grow up, that's what I'm gonna do."

Throughout his childhood, his ambition to fly burned brightly. Joe studied hard in school and did his daily chores with his six brothers on the family farm in Heard County, Georgia, where they raised cotton, corn, cantaloupe, and watermelon. After his father died when Joe was 11, the family moved to the nearby town of Newnan. As a teenager, Joe worked part-time at a Ford garage and wanted to drop out of high school to help support the family. But his mother insisted that he stay in school, telling him, "You need that education for the future."

After graduation, Jackson joined the Army Air Corps (which became the United States Air Force) when he was 18, and earned his wings during World War II. Throughout the Korean War (1950–53), he flew a fighter plane, the F-84 Thunderjet, on 107 combat missions, earning him the Distinguished Flying Cross. He then became one of the first pilots to fly the U-2 spy plane in 1956, and went on to command several reconnaissance detachments around the world.

During service in his third war, he was deployed in 1967 to Vietnam, where he flew the C-123 Provider, a twin-engine, propeller-driven transport that carried troops (as many as

60) and supplies. He had risen in rank to lieutenant colonel and, at age 45, was one of several older C-123 pilots, jokingly called the Grandfather Squadron. As detachment commander for the 311th Air Commando Squadron, Jackson flew once or twice a week. When he flew, it was typically six to eight missions in a day from one base to another, sometimes air-dropping supplies to Special Forces camps that didn't have airstrips.

On Mother's Day 1968 Jackson was on a routine flight, known as a "milk run," when he was ordered to return to his base in the South Vietnamese port city of Da Nang for a briefing about a special mission. Normally he didn't get intelligence briefings because he flew transports, so he knew that whatever the reason, it had to be extremely serious. After arriving in Da Nang, Jackson was told about the crisis in Kham Duc, a camp and village in the central highlands that had been under siege for three days. The troops had put up a valiant defense but were losing the battle to an overwhelmingly large NVA force. As a result, the order was given to completely evacuate Kham Duc at daybreak. Several C-130s — four-engine turbo-prop transport carriers — and the smaller C-123s as well as helicopters were dispatched to the area.

The first to arrive were Army and Marine CH-47 Chinooks, lumbering, dual-prop helicopters. When they dropped through the early-morning fog over Kham Duc, they were met by a strong salvo of enemy fire. One of the big choppers was hit and crashed and burned on the runway. The flaming wreckage blocked the landing area and reduced the 6,000-foot-long airstrip to 2,200 feet, making it challenging for the transport and cargo planes to land safely.

As B-52 bombers and fighter jets began a series of bombing runs to stall the advancing enemy, the Chinooks continued attempts to rescue the trapped American and South Vietnamese troops. Only a few of the choppers managed to get in and out with soldiers onboard.

Members of Company A, 70th Engineer Battalion earlier had dismantled their two large bulldozers to keep the enemy from using the machinery. But after the Chinook crashed, the engineers frantically reassembled one of the bulldozers. By midday, the repaired dozer shoved part of the wreckage off the runway while under constant enemy fire.

Lieutenant Colonel Daryl Cole then landed his C-130, which was immediately swamped by a mob of frightened wives and children of South Vietnamese soldiers. Although his plane was loaded beyond capacity, Cole tried to take off, but shrapnel from enemy mortars and bullets shattered a cockpit window, ripped into the fuselage and wings, tore open a fuel line, and flattened a tire. Forced to abort the takeoff, Cole and his crew unloaded the civilians, moved them to cover, and began cutting away the rubber of the flat tire with a bayonet and blow torch. After replacing the tire, he and his crew loaded the damaged C-130, safely took off, and nursed the plane back to its base.

Meanwhile, Major Ray Shelton brought in his C-123. Despite a shelling from nearly a dozen mortars, he and his crew filled the plane with passengers and made it out.

At 3:25 P.M., Major Bernard Bucher landed his C-130 on the battle-scarred runway where more than 150 people, mostly South Vietnamese civilian women and children, scrambled to get onboard. Once the plane was loaded, it roared down the runway and was met by a barrage of hostile fire. The aircraft began to shake violently out of control, then turned and crashed into a fireball in a nearby ravine. All aboard perished.

After watching Bucher's plane crash, Lieutenant Colonel William Boyd, Jr., tried to land his C-130 in Kham Duc, but couldn't at first because of the heavy concentration of small arms fire. However, he refused to give up. Even though his plane was struck by more than 100 bullets, Boyd landed, quickly boarded about 100 troops, then safely took off. After the transport landed at its base, Boyd's copilot found a can of spray paint and wrote "Lucky Duc" on the side of the plane.

Following Boyd into Kham Duc, Lieutenant Colonel John Delmore's transport was hit repeatedly by automatic weapons fire that ripped out the top of the cockpit, penetrated the floor and the ceiling of the cabin, and shot away the hydraulic-boosted controls. As smoke filled the cockpit and cargo hold, Delmore crash-landed his shot-up plane and managed to steer it clear of the runway before burying the craft's nose into a mound of dirt. The five crewmembers scrambled out of the wreckage. Armed only with their .38 revolvers, they avoided capture and were soon rescued and spirited away by a Marine helicopter.

Meanwhile, airstrikes from American fighter jets were directed at the guns that brought down Bucher's airplane. Other strikes — including napalm and cluster bombs — provided protective cover alongside the runway.

Back in Da Nang, Jackson completed the briefing on the crisis and made preparations to assist in the evacuation. He and his crew — copilot Major Jesse Campbell, flight engineer Technical Sergeant Edward Trejo, and loadmaster Staff Sergeant Manson Grubbs — drew flak vests and extra ammo for their .38 revolvers and brought along an additional M16. By 3 P.M., their C-123, which had the call sign Bookie 771, was airborne for Kham Duc, about 45 miles southwest of Da Nang. Within minutes, the plane joined other rescue aircraft that were circling over the beleaguered base, waiting for a chance to pick up the remaining troops.

Looking out his window, Jackson saw the smoking ruins of downed aircraft on the shortened runway. He also saw a C-130 piloted by Lieutenant Colonel Jay Van Cleef land in heavy fire in an attempt to rescue whatever Americans remained. When no more U.S. troops appeared, Van Cleef revved his engines and flew out of danger. Despite the loss of eight planes and helicopters and the lives of about 200 people, the mission to evacuate Kham Duc had been accomplished. Or so it seemed.

Over the radio, Jackson heard General Burl McLaughlin, commander of the 834th Air Division, order bombers and fighter jets to destroy the camp so the enemy couldn't use it.

But then Van Cleef radioed in a frantic voice, "Negative! Negative! We've still got three airmen on the ground!"

The radio channel, which had been crackling with constant chatter and orders, fell silent for several seconds because everyone was stunned by the news. The order to level the camp was immediately canceled.

Left behind were Major John Gallagher and his two combat controllers, Sergeant Jim Lundie and Technical Sergeant Mort Freedman. They had been dropped off at Kham Duc days earlier to organize and direct aircraft that were delivering troops and supplies into the camp. During the evacuation, the team had guided the rescue planes and choppers in and out of the landing strip, trying to keep the aircraft away from the enemy guns.

Now they were on their own, hiding among the burning buildings and exploding ammo while hundreds of advancing NVA soldiers, who had set up three large machine guns at the airstrip, were closing in. Although the combat controllers were skilled in escape and evasion and hand-to-hand fighting, the odds that they could survive were slim. Making matters worse, the American forces had destroyed all the camp's radios before evacuating so they would be useless to the enemy. There was no way for the trio to communicate with the planes circling above.

The men sought cover in a shallow drainage ditch by the side of the runway, but none of the crew in the rescue aircraft knew where the three were hiding. Braving enemy fire, pilots in a jet fighter and a propeller-driven plane swooped in low trying to spot them, but the trio couldn't be seen.

In his C-123, Lieutenant Colonel Alfred Jeanotte, Jr., radioed to his fellow pilots, "I'm going in for a look." As enemy guns erupted, the bold pilot skillfully landed his defenseless plane and, with mortars exploding around him, rolled down the runway, hoping that at any second, Gallagher, Lundie, and Freedman would sprint out from their hiding place.

But the three combat controllers were busy firing their weapons to keep the enemy at bay. While looking for the men, Jeanotte kept his C-123 moving on the badly damaged airstrip because the plane was getting peppered by machine gun and small arms fire. When he finally spotted the trio, it was too late. Jeanotte had already accelerated to full power and lifted off.

For the men on the ground, it looked as if they had lost their last chance at a rescue. The NVA soldiers turned their focus on the marooned Americans, who were less than 200 yards away.

As he reached a safe altitude, Jeanotte radioed Airborne Command Post (ACP), "I saw the men just as I was taking off. They ran out of a ditch by the side of the runway. I'm running way low on fuel and don't have enough left in the tanks for another landing."

"Is there anyone who can make an attempt to pick them up?" radioed the ACP.

Jackson looked at Campbell, his copilot, and nodded. Campbell knew exactly what that meant, so he got on the radio and said, "Airborne Command Post, this is Bookie 771. We're going in."

Jackson had a good idea of where the men were hiding. As he prepared to make the dangerous rescue attempt, he informed each of his crew exactly what he wanted them to do. He told Campbell, "When we get on the ground, make sure that the flaps get from the assault position [full down] back up to the takeoff position." To Trejo, the flight engineer, Jackson said, "Keep those engines running when we land. I'm going to stop by using brakes only." He told the crew he wouldn't be reversing the propellers on landing because even though it would help slow down the plane, it would also shut off the auxiliary booster jets under the wings. "If we have to start them up again, we'll be sitting ducks," he explained. To Grubbs, the loadmaster, the pilot said, "As soon as this thing touches down, get the doors opened and get those three guys on board as fast as possible."

The veteran pilot surveyed the scene below. A helicopter wreck had dangerously shortened the runway. The airstrip was littered from one end to the other with debris, shell holes, and unexploded ordnance. *The whole thing is a mess,* he thought. Adding to the hazardous conditions, a large thunderstorm was brewing uncomfortably close over the camp.

Jackson wanted to avoid enemy antiaircraft fire as much as possible. From his vantage point, he had seen Jeanotte's plane make a long, low flat approach — standard for a transport — which exposed it to massive enemy fire. *I don't want any part of that,* he thought. *I need to put my plane in a steep dive at a high rate of descent.* He figured that if he cut the power and dropped full flaps, the engines would be so quiet the enemy wouldn't hear them. His plane could be on the ground before the NVA could react. *Get down as quickly as we can and then get out as quickly as we can,* he told himself. *We have only seconds to pull this off.*

He didn't kid himself; he was scared. But he believed fear was a good thing when you're in danger; fear helps you see things a lot clearer so you can make better decisions and react quicker than normal. In fact, he had used fear to his advantage in previous brushes with death — like the time during the Korean War when he barely escaped from getting shot down after his F-84 Thunderjet and three others were attacked by 16 lightning-fast MiGs.

As the tension, anxiety, and excitement built in his body, Jackson felt an uneasy dread that a bullet would come crashing through the cockpit and strike him. It caused him to wonder how long he would feel the pain.

Aw, the heck with it, he told himself, shoving all negative thoughts from his mind. *Let's get on with this flight and save those guys.* He banked his cargo plane to line up with the runway and put the C-123 into a risky steep dive usually executed only by fighter jets. The needle on the instrument gauge that showed how fast the plane was descending was over as far as it would go — a maximum of 5,000 feet per minute. At that rate, the transport was being pushed to the limits of its capability before it potentially could break apart.

But in the hands of an experienced pilot like Jackson, the C-123 performed flawlessly. In less than two minutes, it broke the descent just above the treetops and touched down, triggering a flurry of machine-gun and mortar fire. As the plane barreled down the littered runway at speeds too fast for a normal landing, Jackson fought the controls. He jammed his feet hard on the brakes until the transport slowed down near the drainage ditch where the three men were last seen.

Enemy gunners in the surrounding hills were shooting down at the plane. Jackson saw tracers striking the runway and ricocheting under the C-123. Knowing that the plane's belly sat only about two feet off the ground, the pilot thought, *Boy, they're missing us mighty close.*

As Jackson turned the plane around and revved the engines, Campbell, the copilot, shouted, "There they are!" Gallagher, Lundie, and Freedman sprinted toward the plane in a hail of bullets. Grubbs opened the cargo door and pulled the trio inside.

While Jackson was watching them board in the rear, Campbell yelled, "Oh, my God, look at that!"

Jackson swiveled his head to the front and was startled by what he saw. From the edge of the runway the enemy had fired a 122-mm rocket straight at the transport plane. There was nothing that Jackson or Campbell could do but watch in horror. As the six-foot-long missile zoomed down the airstrip directly at them, it struck the pavement, bounced a few times, and broke in half. The two pieces skidded within 25 feet of the plane's nose before stopping in wisps of smoke. Incredibly, the rocket failed to explode.

Jackson knew that had it blown up, he and Campbell would likely have been killed. When it didn't go off, he told himself, *Fate is on our side. Now I know we're going to get out of here safely. Obviously, everything is being controlled by some power much greater than me.*

Once he received word from Grubbs that the three men were secured, Jackson taxied around the dud rocket, applied power, and headed down the runway through another gauntlet of enemy fire. Within seconds, the sturdy C-123 was airborne. From touchdown to takeoff, the plane was on the ground less than one minute.

As it gained altitude, Grubbs reported to Jackson, "The runway is getting blasted by mortar rounds right where we were ten seconds ago. We came pretty close to getting blown up."

After dodging the thunderstorm that was dumping cascades of rain on the now-abandoned camp, Jackson headed the plane for Da Nang. He felt good, real good. *We did our job and saved those guys.*

On the short flight home, Lundie came up to the flight

deck. "Man, I want to see how big you are when you stand up," he told Jackson.

The pilot gave him a quizzical glance and asked, "Why?"

"Because you must have an awful lot of guts in you to do what you just did."

In the back of the plane, Freedman told the crew, "The thought of another plane was impossible and illogical, because the NVA were moving all around us. So much ammo was blowing up you couldn't tell incoming from our own. I felt if any of the pilots knew we were here, no man in his right mind would attempt a landing. I never felt so lonely in all my life."

Added Lundie, "It didn't seem like there was any possible way for a plane to get in. The whole camp was burning and exploding. When I looked up and saw that C-123 coming in, it was like a miracle. I couldn't believe it. We were dead, and all of a sudden we were alive."

It was getting dark by the time the C-123 touched down at Da Nang. The combat-control trio didn't get a chance to formally thank Jackson and his crew for saving them. Shortly after they had disembarked from the plane, the base was hit by a brutal rocket attack, forcing everyone to dash for the safety of the bunkers. During the siege, the three rescued men got separated from the crew and then, following the all-clear, they hitched a ride to their own base.

When Jackson and Campbell examined their aircraft, they were surprised at how fortunate they were. Despite all the enemy fire and mortar rounds, the two officers couldn't find a single hole from a bullet or shrapnel. Amazingly, the plane came through totally unscathed.

Later, as he settled into his bunk, Jackson remembered it was Mother's Day. He took out a pen and paper and began to write a letter to his wife, Rosamond, the mother of his son and daughter. He wrote, "Dear Rosie. I had an extremely exciting mission today. I can't describe it to you in a letter, but one of these days I'll tell you all about it."

For his actions that day, Joe Jackson was awarded the Medal of Honor by President Lyndon Johnson on January 16, 1969. "I never thought it was that heroic on my part," the humble pilot said. "I was just doing my job."

Jesse Campbell, the copilot, was awarded the Air Force Cross. The other crew members, Edward Trejo and Manson Grubbs, were decorated with the Silver Star. Bernard Bucher, who died when his C-130 went down, was awarded the Air Force Cross, as were William Boyd, the pilot of the "Lucky Duc," and Alfred Jeanotte, who made the first attempt to rescue the combat control team. Daryl Cole, the pilot who flew more than 100 troops out in his badly damaged C-130, and Ray Shelton, who did the same thing in his C-123, each received the Silver Star.

Jackson flew nearly 300 missions in Vietnam, then served in the Pentagon and taught at the Air War College before retiring from the Air Force with nearly 33 years on active duty. He spent the next 11 years working for the Boeing Company, a multinational aerospace and defense corporation. By attending classes nights and weekends, he earned a degree in education at the University of Nebraska at Omaha and a masters in international affairs from George Washington University. He lives with his wife, Rosamond, in Kent, Washington, where once a week he and his friends collect leftover grocery store food and deliver it to a church and a food bank for the needy.

Of the three combat controllers, Jackson never saw or heard from John Gallagher again. Jackson has stayed in touch with Jim Lundie and Mort Freedman through occasional letters. He had an unexpected surprise in 1997 at a race at the Charlotte Motor Speedway in North Carolina after he was introduced to the crowd of 185,000 fans as a Medal of Honor recipient. Lundie, who had left the Air Force in 1968, was in the stands and managed to find his way to Jackson for an emotional reunion. It was the first time the two had seen each other since the dramatic rescue 29 years earlier. "You hear about long-lost family members being reunited and the emotions they feel," Lundie told reporters at the time. "This was the same close family feeling for me."

VALOR AND VENGEANCE

Army Specialist 4th Class Kenneth Stumpf

Squad leader Kenneth Stumpf was walking point — the soldier in front in a seven-man patrol — that was quietly trekking through a rice paddy in a dangerous search-and-destroy mission.

He had walked point many times before, but this day would be different. It would descend into a bloody, chaotic fight where his valor would save other's lives.

When Stumpf was deployed to the jungles of Vietnam in the fall of 1966, none of his fellow soldiers figured the new guy would amount to anything. The 22-year-old draftee from the riverfront town of Menasha, Wisconsin, hadn't exactly inspired confidence during his first few weeks in country.

True, he was gung-ho about the Army. In fact, he had volunteered for the infantry and for service in Vietnam because he felt a debt was owed to the men and women who had served before him. When the helicopter dropped him off in the steamy jungle to join his unit — the 3rd platoon, Company C, 1st Battalion, 35th Infantry, 25th Division — Stumpf tried to make a good first impression: clean-shaven face, spit-shined boots, cleaned and pressed fatigues.

But he seemed nothing like the stubble-faced, sweaty, mud-caked troops who were catching a breather, towels wrapped around their sunburned necks. Most seemed lost in the "thousand-yard stare" — the unfocused gaze of a battle-weary soldier.

When Stumpf looked into their eyes, he thought, *It's like the life has been sucked out of them, like they've been through hell.*

After he and the other newbies lined up, their squad leader, Sergeant Simms, inspected them and snarled, "Who has all that shaving lotion on?"

Stumpf stepped forward and said, "Me, Sergeant."

Simms got in his face and scolded him. "Do you want the enemy to smell you from a mile away and give them our location?" Simms snapped. "Wash that off and don't ever wear that stuff out here again!"

Oh, man, Stumpf fretted, *I've been here for, like, an hour, and I'm already in trouble!*

Two weeks later, he contracted malaria and was hospitalized for more than a month. After he returned, his first taste of combat didn't turn out the way he had envisioned. Because the other troops didn't want to be near a newbie until he could prove he was a good soldier, Stumpf was the last man on a patrol that was tromping through thick jungle. Out of the blue, enemy small arms fire erupted. Panic-stricken, Stumpf began running and got tangled up in vines, and managed to fire only one round before his M16 jammed. Adding to his woes, he didn't know where the enemy was, much less his own platoon. He was so scared that his throat dried up and he couldn't talk. By the time the fighting stopped, he had untangled himself and found his comrades.

Stumpf's first real firefight came a few weeks later at the end of October. He was second in a single-file line, walking on a path on the side of a hill when the enemy conducted a hit-and-run ambush of his squad. The soldier in front and the one behind Stumpf were shot during a ten-second burst of hostile fire. Scared witless, Stumpf dived into the brush for cover and promptly lost his weapon and his helmet. From above, enemy grenades came raining down.

Stumpf was so petrified that he had to fight the urge to run for his life. *There are more bad guys up on the hill than we've got down here,* he told himself. *Where's my rifle? Where's my steel pot?* As he made a frantic search for his equipment in the dense vegetation, he thought, *Maybe I should just run back to the platoon. Oh, man, my heart is beating so fast I can hardly breathe.*

But then he found his weapon and helmet and calmed himself. From his hidden position, he spotted several Viet

Cong running down the trail away from the Americans. He squeezed off several rounds and dropped the enemy soldier who had been covering for them during their withdrawal.

Every day from then on, Stumpf — "Stumpy" to his battle buddies in Charlie Company — gained confidence as a soldier. Within a month, he had shown so much promise he was made a squad leader even though he was only a private first class. By January he had been promoted to specialist 4th class and had earned respect from his comrades for his leadership and smarts during combat.

In April 1967 two new guys joined his squad, William Bush and Anthony Hernandez. Bush was skinny but the tallest man in the unit at six feet, six inches. Shaking Bush's hand when they were introduced, Stumpf thought, *How did they ever put him in the infantry? He's such a big target he won't last long out here.*

A few days later, on the morning of April 25, in Quang Ngai province, Charlie Company came across several enemy bunkers and trenches that showed signs of having been recently occupied by the 2nd Viet Cong Regiment. Moments later, a crewman on a Huey gunship radioed they had opened fire on two enemy soldiers, killing one and wounding the other. The injured VC managed to crawl into a man-made spider hole near Bich Chieu hamlet.

Stumpf, now a jungle veteran of seven months, was ordered to take his seven-man squad and find the wounded soldier. "There's almost certainly going to be trouble ahead," he warned his men. "Stay alert. We'll walk single file and space ourselves about twenty meters apart. I'll take point." The squad leader was supposed to be in the middle, but he felt comfortable walking point, which he did quite often. Even though it was the most dangerous place to be, he wanted to show the two newbies he wouldn't ask his men to do anything he wouldn't do.

Shortly after 11 A.M., the squad began slogging across 400 meters of rice paddies and thick underbrush toward Bich Chieu. A few minutes behind them were Sergeant John Madonich, who had a radio, and his seven-man squad from the 3rd platoon.

Stumpf and his men soon came upon a narrow trail that led to a long trench about two meters wide and one meter deep. Several meters beyond the front of the trench was a thick stand of palm trees and bamboo — a perfect place for the enemy to hide. Before advancing any farther, Stumpf wanted to contact the company commander, Captain Joseph Caudillo.

"Hold the squad here," Stumpf told one of his men, Larry White. "I'm going back up the trail to find Madonich so I can use his radio and ask Caudillo if he wants us to continue."

As Stumpf headed back, the jungle exploded in gunfire behind him. Fearing for his men, he raced toward the trench before dropping to the ground and low-crawling the rest of the way below a curtain of enemy bullets. When he slipped into the trench, he saw only three of his six troops. "Where are the others?" he asked.

"Bush, Hernandez, and White wanted to check out the area to the east of the trench," a soldier replied. "They had moved about twenty meters when a VC gunner got them. They're hurt real bad and they can't walk or crawl. We can't get to them because there's a whole bunker complex out there full of VC."

Stumpf could hear the men crying out in pain and for help. *At least they're still alive,* he thought. He and the three remaining squad members kept their heads down as enemy bullets sprayed inches above them. An RPG exploded behind them, showering them with splinters of tree bark and branches. Stumpf was scared mainly because he couldn't see the enemy through the vegetation. Ignoring his fear, he told himself, *I'm the squad leader of these wounded men, and I've gotta find a way to save them.*

Enemy machine gunners and riflemen hidden in the brush were now directing all their firepower on the Americans' trench. Stumpf and his men kept shooting back and were soon joined by Madonich's squad.

Several camouflaged VC, covered in leaves and branches, tried to sneak up on the Americans from the side. The enemy soldiers — wearing fatigues, pith helmets, and sandals made from old tires — crouched low as they moved silently through the brush. Suddenly, one of Stumpf's men shouted, "The bushes are moving! The bushes are moving!"

At the last moment, the camouflaged VC were spotted and mowed down.

While firing from the trench, Stumpf saw a VC running toward him just as he heard someone shout, "Stumpy, you've got a grenade between your legs!"

Stumpf looked down and saw that it was a "potato masher" — an explosive canister on the end of a wooden handle. There was no one in the trench to his right, so he kicked the grenade about three meters in that direction and ducked. Luckily, the grenade failed to go off. Then he wheeled around and shot the VC who threw it.

Stumpf was trying to figure out how to reach the three wounded men who were nearby but unseen in the dense jungle in front of the trench. *I have to do something,* he told himself. *I've gotta get my guys back. It's the least I can do. They'd do that for me.* Stumpf tried to sneak out of the trench, but was forced back down by intense hostile fire.

Another Viet Cong squad attempted a second flanking movement, running and firing from the hip and throwing grenades. Shrapnel and bullets tore into Stumpf's three men in the trench and several of Madonich's soldiers. They didn't have a medic, so they bandaged one another's wounds. Everyone except Stumpf had been hit, although most were still able to fight.

Frustration and fear set in. *Mom,* Stumpf thought, *I can't believe I'm gonna die in this trench.* He was so scared that he lost all track of time and just kept shooting and hurling grenades.

The fate of the three wounded men preyed on his mind, so he started out of the trench for another rescue attempt. Exposed from the waist up, Stumpf faced a barrage of enemy fire. One of the bullets struck his M16, knocking the weapon out of his hands and sending him backward into the trench. When he retrieved his rifle, it no longer worked because the bullet had destroyed the chamber. *If I hadn't been holding the weapon in front of me, that bullet would've struck me right in the gut,* he thought.

His main concern remained the three wounded soldiers bleeding to death somewhere out there. Above the din of guns and grenades, he could still hear them moaning and begging for help.

"I don't know exactly where they are, but I'm gonna try and save 'em," he told Madonich. "I've been stopped twice before, but this time I'm gonna run through the brush, find 'em, and bring 'em back." Turning to the others in the trench, he said, "Cover me the best you can."

He had no weapon, having tossed aside his useless rifle. It didn't matter because his focus now wasn't on killing his enemies; it was on saving his comrades. As he crept out of the trench, he was so scared, his eyes watered and his mouth went dry. *I'm probably going down but I've gotta try.* He took a deep breath and told himself, *Go! Go! Go!*

Bending over to become a smaller target, the five-foot-five-inch, 119-pound soldier bolted through fierce enemy fire toward the spot where he figured the three men had fallen. During his mad dash, he worried that he would get gunned down. *When is that slug gonna barrel into me?* Legs pumping, Stumpf darted 20 meters and guessed right. He found a depression in the ground where the wounded men were huddled, and he jumped in next to them.

He crawled over to White, who said, "I think my leg is broken. I can't move."

Stumpf scrunched up next to White and rolled on his side so his back was against White's chest. "Grab hold of my neck and I'll put you on my back," Stumpf instructed. "Don't let go."

As adrenaline surged through his body, Stumpf crawled toward the trench with White draped over his back. The VC opened up on the two Americans, but none of the bullets struck the pair. When they reached the front of the trench, their buddies pulled White to safety.

Even though Stumpf was in excellent shape, he was out of breath. Some of that was from exertion; the rest was from fear. But, between gasps, he told his men, "I'm goin' back out again. Cover me." Trying hard to block thoughts of getting killed, he once again braved enemy fire, this time to reach Hernandez, who was in terrible pain and screaming, "Help me! Help me!" He had been shot in the stomach and foot.

Stumpf picked him up and half dragged, half crawled with him toward the trench. Exhausted, Stumpf fell to the ground, rested a few seconds, and then hauled Hernandez to within five meters of the trench before collapsing again. Two fellow soldiers hopped out of the trench and yanked Hernandez in.

Huffing and puffing, Stumpf charged out into the crackling wall of enemy fire to reach Bush, who had been shot in the legs. "Can you walk?" Stumpf asked.

"I think so," Bush replied.

Stumpf grabbed Bush by the collar, drew him to his feet, and, holding his limping comrade by the arm, led him through the kill zone. Dog-tired and wheezing, Stumpf stumbled and fell about ten meters short of the trench. With his buddies urging him on and providing cover, Stumpf helped Bush to safety, completing the remarkable triple rescue. Amazingly, not a single bullet had struck him.

While Bush, Hernandez, and White received medical attention, Stumpf lay on the ground, panting. He was physically burned out. Someone offered him a canteen of water, but he was breathing too hard to drink. What mattered to him was that the men and their weapons had been retrieved. *What a relief!* he thought. *I got my men back to the trench.* But none of the Americans was out of danger because the unrelenting VC kept firing at them.

By now, Stumpf had gone through nearly two dozen grenades, many of which he kept in a sandbag tied to the back of his harness. He now carried someone else's M16, but had emptied most of his original 42 magazines

Stumpf and his men were beginning to run low on ammunition. *We won't be able to hold out much longer,* he thought. Turning to Madonich, he said, "I'm going to run out there and get the weapons and ammo off some of the dead VC. Lay down cover fire for me."

Then he jumped out of the trench and ran from one enemy body to the next, stripping it of ammo and foreign-made automatic rifles. Having slung six enemy guns over each shoulder and carrying ribbons of ammo, he hustled safely back into the trench. With the extra weapons and ammunition, his men were able to fend off the enemy — at least for the moment.

"We've got to get the badly wounded out of here," Madonich told Stumpf. "They've lost a lot of blood, and if they aren't medevacked soon, they'll die."

"There's a rice paddy about forty meters to the rear," Stumpf said. "We can turn that into an LZ [landing zone]."

Acting as rear guard, Stumpf lay down cover fire while the rest moved back, carrying the five most seriously wounded. The able-bodied men set up a perimeter around the rice paddy. By the time Stumpf joined them in a clearing, Madonich had called in a helicopter. Seconds after the chopper landed, the VC blasted away and shattered the windshield, causing the pilot to take off before all of the wounded were put onboard. The helicopter left so quickly that the door gunner, who had jumped off to help load the aircraft, was left behind.

"You're in the infantry now," Stumpf told him.

Madonich called in another chopper, which managed to land and stay on the ground long enough to load the rest of the injured. Although it also was peppered by enemy fire, it lifted off without serious damage.

Meanwhile, the VC were attacking the remaining Americans from two sides. "We gotta get out of here because we can't hold 'em much longer," Stumpf told Madonich. The soldiers ran back toward the trench and set up their defense in a nearby hedgerow.

Stumpf decided it was time to go on the offensive and blow up some of the bunkers. He was getting ready to sneak out when the platoon's artillery forward observer, Private First Class William Latimer, told him, "I'm going with you." A few months earlier at an Army base in Pleiku, Stumpf had knocked him out during a fistfight over which was better — infantry or artillery. But that was all forgotten now.

With Latimer by his side, Stumpf reached the back side of a six-foot-high bunker made out of palm trees and covered with dirt. Stumpf whispered to Latimer, "Cover me." Then Stumpf leaped onto the roof, pulled the pin from a grenade, and tossed it through the opening in the front. After jumping off, he joined Latimer and ducked. A thunderous explosion showered the two men with dirt and debris.

Then they headed for the next bunker. On the way, they turned a corner on a narrow path and encountered four VC. The two Americans each dropped to one knee and fired, killing all four.

As Stumpf started to get up, he felt Latimer fall into him. "Stumpy," Latimer murmured. "I'm dead."

Stumpf saw blood oozing from Latimer's chest. He had been shot through the heart.

Soon the besieged troops were joined by Caudillo's command group, a small unit of six men. Unable to penetrate the enemy's defense, the Americans called in air support. Fighter jets dropped bombs and laid down napalm while gunships raked the area. It was the first time Stumpf had been so close to an air strike of this magnitude, and at one point, he feared the bombs would drop right on him and his buddies. But bomb after bomb struck targets with uncanny precision, knocking down palm trees, wiping out vegetation, and destroying bunkers.

Stumpf and his fellow soldiers discovered that many of the VC surprisingly had survived the aerial attack and were now firing from bunkers that had escaped destruction. However, the remaining bunkers that had been hidden were now exposed, so the Americans were more accurately directing their fire. They were also heartened when they were joined by members of the 2nd platoon.

Another bombing run pummeled the area but still couldn't silence the VC. It was starting to get dark when the raging battle reached the seven-hour mark. Concerned that the enemy would flee, Stumpf told Captain Caudillo, "Sir, we've got to make an infantry charge. If we pull back, they're gonna disappear and we won't get 'em. I know where several bunkers are. I can take 'em out. I just need some more grenades." He had a strong, accurate arm from playing semi-pro baseball back in Wisconsin before he was drafted, so he was confident that he could blow up the bunkers.

After collecting grenades from the other soldiers, Stumpf headed out with Madonich. As the two men crept closer to the enemy, a lone Viet Cong looked out from the slit of a bunker and laughed at Stumpf. Seeing that the foe didn't have a weapon, Stumpf thought, *I've had enough of him.* "You ain't gonna laugh at me no more!" yelled Stumpf, firing off a magazine's worth of bullets into the opening. When Stumpf stopped to change magazines, he couldn't believe his eyes. The same enemy soldier had popped his head up and was laughing at Stumpf again. *I wasted a whole magazine on him,* Stumpf thought. *Well, I'm not squandering any more ammo.* He turned his weapon to the right and shot several VC emerging from the brush.

With Madonich covering him, Stumpf crept up to the side of a bunker where enemy gunners had been firing through an opening that was one foot high and eight feet long. Waiting until they pulled their guns inside, Stumpf boldly ran in front of the bunker, pulled the pin on a grenade, and flung it into the slit.

When he turned around, he was shocked to see that someone had thrown the grenade back out. *Oh, no! I'm going to get blown up!* He dived into the dirt a split second before the grenade exploded in a deafening roar. For a few seconds, Stumpf heard nothing, then only loud ringing in his ears. Fortunately, he wasn't hurt.

Even though he was shaky, he tried again. This time, he pulled the pins of two grenades, released the levers so they were activated, but he held them. Knowing that a grenade is supposed to blow up in three to five seconds after it's activated, he let them "cook" for a couple of seconds. *The VC won't throw these back out,* he told himself. Then he ran in front and threw the grenades inside. He was two strides beyond the bunker when it exploded to smithereens.

Next, Stumpf started sprinting 30 meters to another bunker. Several VC in a hedgerow to his right opened fire on him as streams of blue tracer rounds whizzed by him. Undeterred, he destroyed the bunker with another perfectly thrown grenade.

The Americans who watched Stumpf's rampage left their positions and began advancing. Soon they were no longer met with any hostile fire, because the Viet Cong either had died or had fled the area. The fight near Bich Chieu was over.

After a perimeter was set up at nightfall, Stumpf — his uniform ripped and drenched in sweat — lay on the ground. He was physically and mentally wiped out, his body as listless as a rag doll. *If the VC attack, they can just go ahead and shoot me,* he thought. *I have no energy left.*

But then he was summoned by Captain Caudillo, who told him, "A platoon of ours is in one of the trenches, and they're lost. You know better than anyone the location of the major trenches and remaining bunkers. I need you to find the men and bring them back."

You've gotta be kidding me, Stumpf thought, wondering where he would find the strength. He soon caught his second wind, but he was terrified because it was dark outside and he had to go in the dangerous bunker complex — one that still might be crawling with VC — and locate the lost platoon and guide it to safety. *They know I'll be coming, but they don't know where I am or which direction I'll be coming from. But Captain Caudillo asked for me because he knew I was the best man for the job. Geez, I'm scared, but I gotta do this.*

He picked up a radio and called the lieutenant of the lost platoon. "Put somebody out front that isn't all jumpy and trigger-happy," Stumpf instructed. "We might be in opposite trenches, which could start a firefight with ourselves if you have a guy who begins shooting the minute he hears something."

Stumpf selected four men to go with him and led them in the darkness. Once again he was walking point, this time fretting that he might stumble upon the enemy or get shot by friendly fire. His unit hiked past several empty bunkers, but found no sign of the lost platoon. Eventually, he heard metal clacking, the kind of sound a soldier's equipment makes when he's walking. Stumpf stopped, his heart pounding as he wondered whether it was friend or foe. *Ken, what are you gonna do? You know you won't shoot first in case it's the platoon. They'll have to shoot you first. But what if it's the enemy?*

The sound grew a little louder. *They're coming closer.* Then, in the moonlight, he recognized the outline of a steel pot on a person about five meters away. Because no password had been arranged, he had to say something, so the first words that came to mind were the most obvious: "Are you Americans?"

To his relief, he heard, "Yeah, we are." He then guided the 25 men from the lost platoon back to the company perimeter.

It had been a day when Specialist 4th Class Kenneth Stumpf had given everything he had and then some. As he finally lay down his weary body and closed his tired eyes, he thought, *At least for today, I was the best soldier and warrior that I could possibly be.*

A week after the battle, Captain Joseph Caudillo wrote up an official report recommending that Kenneth Stumpf be awarded the Medal of Honor. A day later, Caudillo led Charlie Company into a rice paddy where they were attacked by the Viet Cong. Seconds after trading places with a lieutenant who was using a palm tree for cover, Caudillo was fatally shot in the head.

VALOR AND VENGEANCE

In September 1967, Stumpf, who was promoted to staff sergeant, was discharged from the Army and returned to his old job at the Banta Printing Company in Menasha, Wisconsin. The following year, on September 19, 1968, President Lyndon Johnson presented the Medal of Honor to Stumpf, who was accompanied by his parents, siblings, and their spouses.

At the urging of the Army, Stumpf reenlisted and served another tour in Vietnam. He suffered his first and only combat wound from grenade shrapnel while the platoon he was leading assaulted an enemy position. He remained in the Army and retired as a sergeant major in the fall of 1994 after 29 years of service.

Today, Stumpf, the father of three and grandfather of six, lives with his wife, Dorothy, in Tomah, Wisconsin.

SAVING SPOOKY 71
Air Force Airman First Class John Levitow

Twenty seconds.

John Levitow knew that's how much time he had left to prevent the crippled attack cargo plane from blowing up, killing him and his seven fellow airmen.

Moments earlier, an enemy mortar round had struck the plane, tearing open a three-foot-wide hole in the right wing and sending thousands of pieces of shrapnel rocketing through the fuselage. Some of the shrapnel had ripped into Levitow and the three crewmen who were with him in the cargo bay, leaving them severely wounded.

Now, as the pilot and copilot struggled to keep the wobbling plane from crashing into the jungle, Levitow was caught up in a much greater drama in the rear. An armed flare was rolling loose on the floor, timed to go off within seconds.

If it ignited, it would trigger an unstoppable series of deadly consequences. Poisonous smoke would fill the aircraft, incapacitating the entire crew. The flare would burn at a temperature of 4,000 degrees Fahrenheit — an intense heat that would melt through the aluminum floor and destroy the control cables underneath. The heat would also cook off the thousands of rounds of ammunition stored in the cargo bay, causing bullets to explode everywhere. The end result: Any one of those events would spell doom for the plane and its crew.

Levitow realized if there was any chance to stop this disaster, he had to reach the elusive flare and toss it out the open cargo door. But he was too hurt to walk. Bleeding badly from more than three dozen shrapnel wounds, he crawled toward the flare, which was rolling from one side of the floor to the other in the swaying plane.

Now there were ten seconds left. Just when he extended his arm to grab the flare, it moved out of his reach. He tried again and again until time had nearly run out.

The 23-year-old airman first class was a crewmember aboard an AC-47 gunship. The twin-engine, propeller-driven former transport plane was outfitted with three mounted 7.62-mm Gatling miniguns that each fired out of an open port on the left side of the fuselage at the rate of 3,000 to 6,000 rounds per minute.

The AC-47 (the AC stands for attack cargo plane) was designed to provide armed support for ground troops at night. Equipped with thousands of rounds of ammo, the plane would circle overhead during a firefight and blast away at the enemy. It also carried up to five dozen MK-24 magnesium flares to illuminate the battlefield, denying the enemy the protection of darkness. When activated and dropped out of the plane on a little parachute, each flare turned night into day for a square mile with an intensity of two million candlepower for up to three minutes before burning out.

In recognition of their nighttime job, the dozens of Air Force AC-47s had a call sign that began with the name Spooky. They were often referred to as "Dragonships" because superstitious Vietnamese saw flashes spewing from the planes' weapons at night and thought the gunships looked like fire-breathing dragons. American troops nicknamed the planes "Puff, the Magic Dragon," which was the title of a hit song in the early 1960s.

Typically, the AC-47 carried a crew of eight — pilot, copilot, navigator, and South Vietnamese officer in the forward cabin; flight engineer, loadmaster, and two gunners in the cargo bay in the back.

Levitow, who was born and raised in Connecticut, enlisted in the Air Force in June 1966. Two years later, he was assigned to the 3rd Special Operations Squadron of the

14th Operations Wing at Bien Hoa Air Base, a few miles northwest of Saigon. The unit flew four missions each night. Spooky 71 and Spooky 73 worked the 6 P.M.-to-midnight shift to search for and destroy the enemy, while Spooky 72 and Spooky 74 flew the midnight-to-dawn stint.

On February 24, 1969, Levitow, who had been in-country for eight months, boarded Spooky 71 for his 181st mission. Because he was filling in for a loadmaster who had taken his place days earlier when he was sick, Levitow had never flown with this crew before. The pilot, Major Kenneth Carpenter, was making his first combat mission as aircraft commander.

Once it was in the air, Spooky 71 began flying a combat air patrol circuit over an area around Saigon and Tan Son Nhut. For the next four-and-a-half hours, the crew kept responding to calls for fire support because the Viet Cong and North Vietnamese soldiers were attacking several American positions. These outposts were coming under heavy mortar and rocket salvos from concealed nighttime positions. But Spooky 71 dropped flares that exposed enemy positions, and its guns directed devastating fire on the VC and NVA troops.

Flying at an airspeed of about 140 mph from an altitude of 3,000 feet, Spooky 71 orbited hour after hour over various enemy positions and let loose with its three miniguns, which Carpenter fired by remote control. The gunners kept the weapons — capable of collectively hitting every square yard of a football field in ten seconds — loaded and functioning properly.

As the loadmaster, Levitow worked with a gunner, Airman First Class Ellis Owen, in a smooth two-man operation to release the flares. Levitow would go to a special rack and pick up a flare — a 27-pound, three-foot-long canister that was nearly six inches in diameter. He would set a timer and fuse delay before handing the canister to Owen. While standing by the open cargo door, Owen would attach a ten-foot-long lanyard (a cord) to a safety pin ring on the canister and wait for the command from the pilot to toss the canister out of the plane. When the canister had fallen beyond the length of the lanyard, it would yank out the safety pin ring, arming the flare. The timer that Levitow had set allowed a ten-second delay before a small charge would release a parachute to slow the canister's descent to the ground. Ten seconds later, the fuse delay would ignite the magnesium, creating an intense light.

About 11:30 P.M., a half hour before Spooky 71's shift was scheduled to end, the crew was ordered to fly over the army base at Long Binh, which was under siege by an enemy force attacking the south and east perimeters. With flares lighting up the ground, Carpenter fired away, taking out two mortar batteries and forcing the enemy to retreat.

But soon the crewmen spotted the flashes of another mortar battery about a mile south. Dropping down to 1,000 feet, Carpenter banked his gunship to the left and began his run on the new mortar positions. In the cargo bay, Levitow had removed another flare from the rack, set the timer, and passed it to Owen, who had hooked the lanyard on the canister and kept his finger on the safety pin ring.

As Owen waited for word to throw out the canister, a brilliant flash momentarily blinded the crewmen. It was followed a fraction of a second later by a loud explosion that violently shook the plane. Levitow, Owen, and the other two in the cargo bay were slammed against the floor and the sides of the fuselage like dice in a tumbler.

In a one-in-a-million-chance happening, Spooky 71 had flown into the path of an 82-mm mortar round, which struck the top of the right wing, splitting open a three-foot-wide gash and puncturing the wing and fuselage with more than 3,500 shrapnel holes. As the shock wave from the blast swept through the inside of the plane, 40 pieces of hot shrapnel and flying metal ripped into the right side of Levitow's body. Dozens of metal shards riddled Owen as well as Sergeant Thomas Baer, who was the other gunner, and Staff Sergeant Edward Fuzie, the flight engineer.

Levitow felt as if an invisible force had bashed him on the right side with a two-by-four, a large piece of lumber. The shrapnel had peppered his legs and back, creating wounds that were starting to bleed badly. His ears, which had been ringing from the blast, were now assaulted by the shrill sounds of the wind shrieking through the thousands of punctures in the fuselage.

The flash from the explosion had lit up the inside of the forward cabin like daylight and played havoc with the instruments and controls. Although Carpenter, the copilot, the navigator, and the South Vietnamese officer weren't struck by shrapnel, they were jarred by the blast.

After it was struck, the plane veered sharply downward and to the right. Struggling to maintain control, Carpenter knew his aircraft had suffered major damage and was in danger of crashing, so he and the copilot worked feverishly to keep the lurching plane in the air.

In the cargo bay, Levitow was stunned from being thrown to the floor by the concussive force of the explosion. With serious wounds to their necks and backs, Owen and Fuzie were dazed and barely moving. As Levitow tried to regain control of his senses, he noticed that Baer was unconscious, covered in blood and lying perilously close to the open cargo door. Because the plane was still rocking wildly from side to side, Levitow feared that, at any moment, Baer could slide right out the doorway to certain death.

Determined to save his fellow airman, Levitow tried to stand, but his right leg was numb, and the pain from his wounds was intensifying. He gritted his teeth, pulled himself up, and staggered toward Baer while the plane continued to wobble. Bracing his arm against the inside of the fuselage, he was barely able to maintain his balance as he worked his way to the unconscious airman. When he was a few feet from the open doorway, Levitow was aware that one jerk of the plane in the wrong direction or angle could fling both him and Baer to their doom. But his focus was on getting Baer out of immediate danger, so Levitow grabbed Baer by the shirt, backpedaled, and dragged him safely away from the door.

Becoming weaker by the second from loss of blood, Levitow wanted to rest. But he couldn't — not when he recognized a hazard that he knew could ultimately destroy the plane. A flare had been activated and was emitting dense blue smoke. It was the one that he had set the timer and fuse delay for and given to Owen moments before Spooky 71 was hit. When Owen had been thrown to the floor by the explosion, the 27-pound canister had tumbled out of his hands. His finger had been on the safety ring pin, so when the canister fell, the pin had been released, arming the flare.

Levitow figured he had less than 20 seconds to seize it and hurl it out of the door before it detonated and turned the aircraft into a blazing torch. But the canister was rolling loose on the floor between one of the miniguns and a stack of cans containing 20,000 rounds of ammunition. Because the canister was banging from one side of the fuselage to the other, Levitow wondered if the main timer had been damaged. There was no way to know if it would go off sooner or later than the time he had set.

The flare was now within his grasp. Just as he reached for it, the plane lurched, causing the canister to move away from him. Feeling light-headed from the loss of blood and in agony from his wounds, Levitow still found the strength to go after the elusive flare. His outstretched hand was about to grip it when the plane made a sharp banking turn, sending the canister rolling again.

With time running out, the desperate airman kept trying. As he closed in on the flare for a third time, he threw his body onto the canister, pinning it to the floor. His arms too weak to pick it up and his legs too numb to walk, Levitow clutched the canister against his chest and crawled toward the open door. He knew that at any second, the flare could explode, killing him instantly in a fiery death while the rest of the crew would face the horror of dying in a flaming crash.

Leaving a trail of blood as he dragged the heavy canister toward the rear, Levitow ignored the pain, and with a gutsy willpower he didn't know he possessed, he reached the open cargo door. Then he mustered all the remaining strength he had and shoved the canister out into the night.

There wasn't a second to spare. Just as the canister cleared the doorway, the flare exploded in a white-hot blaze.

Levitow had saved Spooky 71 from disaster — at least for the moment. In the cockpit, Carpenter was still battling for control of the aircraft. Among other serious issues, aviation gas was leaking from the fuel lines on the right side, causing the pilot to wonder if he could coax the barely flyable gunship back to the base before it fell out of the sky. Carpenter refused to consider ordering his men to bail out, because some crewmembers were too injured to jump. No, they would all survive together or die together.

Those who weren't wounded prepared for a likely crash landing. After a momentary breather, Levitow found the energy to help secure the cargo bay. Standing unsteadily, he stuffed 140-pound cans of ammunition between the mini-guns so the cans wouldn't fly around the fuselage and further injure the crewmen. After completing the task, Levitow was in such physical misery that he passed out.

Its engines sputtering and airspeed near stalling, Spooky 71 approached the base at Bien Hoa. A few hundred yards short of the runway was an old French minefield that was fenced off by barbed wire and had never been cleared of mines. Carpenter's biggest worry was that the plane wouldn't remain airborne long enough to fly over the mine-field; landing short would be catastrophic for everyone on board.

Putting his flying skills to the ultimate test, Carpenter set the aircraft down in a full shuddering stall, just a few yards short of the runway but well past the minefield. Because of shrapnel from the mortar explosion, the right tire was flat from a gash, so when the plane landed, it veered down the runway, forcing Carpenter to stand on the left brake to maintain control. Believing the aircraft could burst into flames from the leaking fuel, Carpenter didn't taxi to the ramp. He stopped the plane on the runway and ordered the crew to evacuate immediately. Everyone, including

Levitow and Baer, who had both regained consciousness, got out safely.

Alerted by an earlier call from the pilot, an ambulance and a medevac helicopter met the crew on the runway. At first, Levitow declined to board the chopper, but Carpenter ordered him to get on with the other wounded airmen. Levitow was flown to the Air Force hospital at Tachikawa, Japan, where 40 pieces of shrapnel were removed between his knee and his hip. He spent more than two months recuperating in Japan before returning in April to Vietnam, where he flew 20 more combat missions during the next four months. He then finished his three-year military commitment and was honorably discharged from the Air Force with the rank of sergeant.

Shortly after that fateful February night in 1969, Carpenter nominated Levitow for the Medal of Honor. In his statement of recommendation, the major said, "Others were there, others were wounded, but Levitow being the farthest removed from the flare, recognized the danger, took action when seconds counted, and saved the lives of the entire crew. Levitow's progress was clearly marked with his own blood on the floor of the aircraft."

The Medal of Honor was presented to Levitow at the White House by President Richard Nixon on May 14, 1970, which happened to be Armed Forces Day. Levitow was the first enlisted man in the Air Force to receive the award. A modest man, he told reporters later, "I'm just lucky. I'm sure there are many people who have served who have done things that have been simply amazing and never been recognized."

Said Carpenter at the time, "I'll never know how Levitow managed to get to the flare and throw it out," because of the way Spooky 71 was pitching and rolling after it was hit. "In my experience, I have never seen such a courageous act performed under such adverse conditions. The entire eight-man crew owes their lives to John, and his quick reactions surely saved the aircraft."

After John Levitow left the Air Force, he worked for federal and state veterans' affairs agencies for more than 22 years, including nine years as a liaison between the Veterans Administration and Congress. He was married and had a son and a daughter.

The Air Force has never forgotten Levitow's heroics. The top graduate of each Air Force Airman Leadership School receives the Levitow Honor Graduate Award. The training group headquarters building at Lackland Air Force Base in Texas is named for him. He is remembered at the Walk of Fame at Hurlburt Field in Florida. In a ceremony at Long Beach, California, in 1998, the Air Force named a C-17 Globemaster plane after him, the first time ever that such an honor was given to an enlisted man. The legend on the fuselage reads: "The Spirit of Sgt. John L. Levitow."

Levitow died on November 8, 2000, at his home in Rocky Hill, Connecticut, after a lengthy battle with cancer. He was

55. When he was buried at Arlington National Cemetery a week later, more than 500 airmen attended the funeral. At the ceremony, Chief Master Sergeant of the Air Force Jim Finch said, "John Levitow for years has been woven into the fabric of enlisted heritage. Through his heroic efforts, he was the embodiment of our core value 'service before self.' His name has become synonymous with excellence, and his legacy will continue to live in the hearts and minds of all Air Force members today and well into the future."

Levitow had willed his Medal of Honor to the Enlisted Heritage Research Institute at the Senior Noncommissioned Officer Academy at Maxwell Air Force Base in Gunter Annex, Alabama. On display at the facility's Enlisted Heritage Hall are Levitow's medal, uniform, ribbons, photos, and other memorabilia, including the original Medal of Honor citation signed by President Nixon. Visitors can watch a videotape of Major Carpenter and John Levitow, Jr., talking about the Medal of Honor mission. Outside the Enlisted Heritage Hall is an old C-47 that was converted into a replica of Spooky 71, complete with a mannequin of Levitow struggling to drag the flare to the open cargo door.

Levitow's hometown of Glastonbury, Connecticut, dedicated a memorial to him on the town green in 2004. Among the family members present were his son, John Levitow, Jr., and grandson, John Levitow III.

"WE STILL HAVE FIGHT IN US!"

Marine Captain James Livingston

Fix bayonets now!"

Captain James Livingston had never issued such an order before. But he knew those three words would get his troops psyched for what was gearing up to be the most challenging battle of their lives — and his.

The men under his command — Company E, 2nd Battalion, 4th Marines — understood the significance of fixing bayonets onto their rifles: It meant prepare for close-in fighting, including hand-to-hand combat, against a strong enemy force. It meant drop your gear, take off your packs, and leave everything you don't need behind. It meant carry nothing but your weapons, magazines, ammo, and Ka-Bars (military-issue knives).

Hearing the distinctive steel-on-steel clicks of 180

bayonets locking into place onto their M16s, the 28-year-old officer knew his men were primed. Those leathernecks had never let him down. They had been in daunting situations before. Under his leadership, they had never lost a fight and he was darn sure they weren't going to lose this one, either, no matter the odds, no matter the risks.

That wasn't always the case. Nine months earlier, when Livingston was handed command of Company E (also called Echo Company), it was a ragtag unit that had become dispirited after losing half its men in combat. Morale had sunk to rock bottom. Emotionally and mentally beaten down, some of the men were flabby and ailing. Many suffered from immersion foot, a painful condition caused by failure to keep feet dry after slogging through the warm water in rice paddies.

What they needed, the new captain decided, was some good, old-fashioned tough love — and he was going to give it to them.

Long before enlisting in the Marines, Livingston had developed a solid work ethic and deep respect for discipline fashioned by his parents while growing up on a farm in south Georgia. He applied those same traits in college, graduating from Auburn University with a degree in civil engineering before entering the military.

Reflecting the characteristics he learned from his father — who was as demanding as any drill sergeant — Livingston forced his men to snap out of their funk and start acting and looking like Marines. "The way you look demonstrates the way you will react," he told his men. "If you look shaggy, you fight shaggy. If you're out of shape, you can't perform your duties. If your weapons are dirty, you can't use them. If your feet are hurting, you can't fight."

He got them fit again through rigorous PT — physical training that he often led — and a regimen of good hygiene along with a proper diet. He made them clean their weapons daily and trained them in new combat techniques. As he rebuilt the unit, he kept motivating and inspiring them until they regained confidence in themselves and became a determined, cohesive fighting force.

Leading by example, Livingston always shaved, kept his hair buzz-cut, wore a clean uniform, and had his gear in order — and expected no less from his men. Whether it was a PT run or a firefight, they could always count on their steadfast captain to be out in front. He never stopped pushing the troops to be better, telling them, "There's no such thing as reaching your peak." Even when they were out in the field, he insisted they train, do their daily PT, get their haircuts, and wear clean uniforms.

Over the months, his leadership, along with the experience from several brutal battles, had sharpened his men. He had prepared them physically and mentally, taking them to a combat level of high expectations. Above all, he wanted them so disciplined and well trained that they would come home alive.

By the spring of 1968, the captain had turned Echo Company into a top-notch unit. At the end of April, the men were providing security on a strategic bridge over the Cua Viet River just north of Dong Ha, a major Marine resupply base. They had to defend the bridge and a section of the river against NVA forces, which were pressing down from the north, trying to choke off the Americans' water-supply route.

While his company was protecting the bridge on April 30, Livingston was monitoring the reports of a vicious battle raging two kilometers away, in and around the village of Dai Do. He could hear the fighting and see the smoke. His fellow leathernecks there were suffering heavy casualties and getting bogged down against an enemy force much larger than anticipated. Chomping at the bit for Company E to join the fight, Livingston urged his superiors to release his men from guarding the bridge, but he was told to stick with his orders because there was no unit available to replace his. *I feel like a junkyard dog tied to a leash,* he thought. *My brothers are fighting and dying out there, and I can't do a thing about it.*

On the afternoon of May 1, supply trucks loaded with food, including steaks, fresh fruit, and soft drinks, arrived at Echo Company's position. The delivery, arranged earlier by Livingston as a reward for his men, was a rare treat, especially in the field. They were ready to sit down to a steak dinner — their first hot meal in days — when Livingston finally received orders for his unit to mount up and hustle toward An Lac, a village near Dai Do, as needed reinforcements.

On the way there, Company E was harassed by marauding bands of NVA scouts who repeatedly fired on them, killing several Marines. Rather than pursue the scouts, Livingston kept his men marching toward An Lac as quickly as possible.

When they reached a swift stream that was more than five feet deep in some places, the captain came up with a clever way to ford it. On his orders, a half dozen of his tallest men stripped down, planted themselves in the deepest part of the stream, and passed the shorter Marines hand to hand until they reached shallow water. Although the men were soaked, their weapons and ammo remained dry. By 7 P.M., Echo Company had reached An Lac, becoming the fourth rifle company of the 800-man 2nd Battalion, which was facing off against a force at least ten times larger.

Throughout the night, Livingston remained in radio communication with Captain Jay Vargas, commander of Company G (also called Golf Company), a unit that had been chewed up by the NVA and pinned down outside Dai Do. Because of injury and death, only a third of the unit remained combat effective. All but surrounded, Captain Vargas and his 45 surviving Marines were now dug in for the night in a ditch. In addition to their own firepower, they had the support of artillery to hold back the enemy.

"WE STILL HAVE FIGHT IN US!"

At 3 A.M. on May 2, Livingston, who had no sleep, was given his company's mission: Break through the enemy's line of defense, link up with Company G, and secure Dai Do. Based on the high number of Marines killed and seriously wounded in the previous day's battle, the captain figured this mission could be one of the deadliest of his military career.

To impress upon his men the likelihood of close combat and the difficulty of going across 500 meters of open rice paddies under intense enemy fire, he issued an order for the first time to his men: "Fix bayonets now!" *They know it's for real,* he thought. *They know they won't let their buddies down, the other companies down, the Marine Corps down. These kids will do a great job.*

By 4:45 A.M., his men were ready. As a captain, Livingston understood how important it was for an officer to lead his men into battle from up front. "You gotta smell the gunpowder," he always said. "If you can't smell it, you're too far back."

With his radioman by his side, Livingston led Company E into the fog-shrouded rice paddies at dawn. Over the first 300 meters, the leathernecks met little resistance, only occasional shots from a sniper's rifle. But from their hidden entrenched positions, the NVA were patient, letting the Marines move closer and closer.

Suddenly, the enemy unleashed everything they had. Popping up from behind hedgerows, bunkers, trench lines, and spider holes, they raked the battlefield with small arms, automatic rifle, and RPG fire. The Americans threw everything they could bear against their foes — artillery, mortar, helicopter gunships — trying to soften them up. The tremendous noise from all the gunfire, explosions, and low-flying jets forced the Marines to shout at one another from a few feet away just to be heard.

Most of the enemy RPGs were aimed at anything resembling a radio antenna, because the men carrying radios were usually with the commander — in this case, Livingston. Because he was a priority target, the NVA pounded his position. When the first rounds came in, the captain and his command team dived for cover behind one of the many old burial mounds that dotted the rice paddies. Zeroing in on the burial mound that was protecting Livingston, the enemy fired 18 successive rockets, destroying most of it. One RPG slammed into the front of the mound and burrowed nearly all the way through.

Although Echo Company was momentarily slowed down, Livingston concentrated on two goals: accomplish the mission and bring as many Marines back alive as he could. To reach Golf Company and Dai Do, he and his men first needed to destroy about 100 NVA bunkers — a challenge fraught with risk. Most of the bunkers were hidden and built like small A-frames, and strong enough to withstand the weight of a tank. In fact, many withstood American bombs, artillery, napalm, and mortars.

"WE STILL HAVE FIGHT IN US!"

Livingston realized the only way to destroy the bunkers was for his men to get next to them and fling grenades inside to blow them up. However, enemy soldiers who were defending the well-concealed bunkers were almost invisible until the Americans were right on top of them, making the Marines easy targets. Leathernecks were falling at an alarming rate, often from head shots at close range.

Advancing through thick vegetation and nine-foot-tall hedges, Company E was getting hit from the front and the left by NVA soldiers blasting away with their AK-47s. Some sprang from their hiding places and engaged surprised Marines in hand-to-hand combat. Grenades tossed by both sides blew up in thunderous roars, killing friendlies and foes alike.

In the heat of the battle, Livingston continued to encourage his men. "Forward! Forward! Keep moving!" he shouted above the din. Even when things looked bad, he made them believe they would win.

But then a grenade exploded nearby, hurtling a jagged piece of hot metal into his right leg, barely missing a major artery. The captain buckled and then had a corpsman wrap a bandage around the wound to stop the bleeding. Livingston got to his feet and led another charge until he was felled a second time by shrapnel from a grenade blast. Badly wounded, he still carried on.

With his ever-depleting reserve platoon right behind him, the unyielding captain headed straight into enemy fire,

141

driving right up the middle and into the entrenched NVA lines. When his two assault platoons received heavy casualties and lost momentum, he limped back and directed them forward, continuing the attack. Using grenades and M79 grenade launchers, his Marines cleared enemy positions meter by bloody meter until they finally reached Company G. During those previous harrowing hours when Golf Company had been isolated from the rest of the battalion, Vargas had rallied his troops to drive off three NVA attacks. Now together, the two units moved into Dai Do.

The Marines assaulted neck-deep bunkers, fighting holes, gun pits, and connecting trenches that had been cleverly woven into the hedgerows and thickets. Fields of fire overlapped. While trying to destroy one bunker, the Marines were taking fire from another. By teams and pairs, the Americans were throwing grenades, then flanking each bunker and firing into the trench. Some enemy soldiers broke and ran, but most died in place. Although the Marines were sustaining an increasing number of casualties, Livingston had them in a rhythm, steadily plowing forward.

Wielding his .45-caliber M3 grease gun, a lightweight submachine gun, the captain dropped about a dozen enemy soldiers before his weapon jammed. Given an older model M14 automatic rifle, he continued his rampage. Combat was furious . . . and so was his men's fighting spirit.

Private First Class Marshall Serna boldly stood up and blasted his M60 machine gun at the enemy emplacements until he burned out the barrel of his weapon. When three wounded comrades were trapped by enemy fire, he sprinted across the hazardous ground by throwing hand grenades and then helped move the men to a safer place. Seizing another machine gun, he advanced on a trench but was seriously wounded in the leg by a grenade hurled by an enemy soldier in a spider hole. Before losing consciousness, he killed the NVA soldier. Serna's actions (which would later earn him a Silver Star) allowed the platoon to sweep into the right flank of the village and establish a base of covering fire.

At no time did Livingston think he and his men would fail. It wasn't in his DNA or in Echo Company's. *We've never lost a fight . . . and we never will,* he told himself. Seeing his Marines falling by the dozens, the captain persevered. *The best thing I can do for them is to take the objective and medevac the wounded.*

By 9 A.M., Livingston radioed the command post that Dai Do was secured and the enemy had been pushed out. But minutes later, the NVA launched a 15-minute artillery barrage to remind the Americans the battle was still ongoing. Despite his painful injuries, Livingston coordinated the moving of the wounded and the recovery of the dead. Gear and weapons, both the Marines' and the enemy's, were collected and stockpiled. After adding up the casualties, Livingston discovered that his company had only 35 men who could still fight. Eighteen had been killed and more than one hundred had been wounded; the most serious were helicoptered out.

Losing so many troops bothered him. But, he thought, *We had to do what our leadership expected us to do. We rescued Golf Company from getting wiped out.* He told his surviving troops, "You carried out the mission superbly, and unfortunately many paid the ultimate price. We're depleted but not beaten. We still have fight in us! Even though you've done a great job, the fight is not over. We have to be ready to go again at a moment's notice." First, though, he made sure his exhausted men were given plenty of water, food, and ammunition.

Just before 10 A.M., Company H (also called Hotel Company), which had 80 men, headed out toward the next village, Dinh To, to secure it. They advanced only a few hundred meters before the enemy launched a counterattack, sending wave after wave of soldiers against the overmatched Marine unit.

Monitoring the combat on the battalion radio, Livingston heard Hotel Company was drawing heavy fire from the front and both flanks and was in serious danger of being surrounded. *Hotel just walked into a death trap,* the captain thought. *It sounds like a total wipeout of that company if they don't get reinforcements right now.* He radioed his superior officer and said, "Hotel is really fixing to get in trouble. Echo is going to help them."

Without waiting for a response, Livingston told his men, "Pack up right now. Hotel is in trouble, and we need to get to them." Without hesitation, they grabbed their gear and shoved off. In his bloody uniform, Livingston led his company through small clusters of NVA positions, killing the enemy on the run.

After battling their way to Company H's position, Livingston directed the merged companies in a charge against the numerically superior NVA forces, turning the battlefield into a chaotic scene of hand-to-hand fighting. Joining the struggle was Captain Vargas, who was suffering from several earlier wounds, and his dwindling number of men from Company G.

During combat, Livingston took quick glances at his men. *My Marines are holding on with their last breath, but the enemy isn't letting up,* he thought. Firing at NVA positions, he told himself, *Never let the enemy fall back and catch his breath. Choke the life out of him, hit him hard, and hit him often until he collapses.* Marines with jammed or empty weapons gathered anything they could find on the battlefield and kept taking the fight to the enemy.

Many NVA soldiers who were camouflaged in leaves and branches leaped out of their hiding places in the brush and rushed the Americans. Corporal Richard Britton was attacked in close combat by four NVA soldiers bent on killing him. During the struggle, he suffered a slashing wound to his left thigh. Undeterred, he shot one with his Colt .45 and another with his M16. He bayoneted the third man in the throat and killed the last one with his Ka-Bar. Britton was hobbling forward when he was struck by shrapnel from a grenade blast and passed out. (He was rescued and eventually earned the Silver Star for his actions.)

The Americans were making good progress until the NVA cut loose with an ear-shattering display of firepower from within 50 meters. For the next hour, the Marines slugged it out from trench line to trench line while fending off the NVA to their flank. But under tremendous pressure, the Marines could advance no farther. Livingston had to evacuate the dead and wounded, deal with being outnumbered and outflanked, and reorganize his men.

Bravely defying the enemy's onslaught, Livingston stood in the open, firing his rifle at an NVA position where a 12.7-mm machine gun was shooting at U.S. gunships. Suddenly, the enemy turned the antiaircraft gun on Livingston. One of the bullets tore into his right leg, skirting the bone but creating a big hole. The captain went down hard. Rushing to his side, a corpsman threw a tourniquet around Livingston's leg and gave him a morphine tablet for pain. "You're lucky, sir," the medic said. "If that round had struck the bone, it would have cut off your entire leg."

"WE STILL HAVE FIGHT IN US!"

"Go on and help someone else," Livingston ordered. He noticed some panic in the eyes of his younger troops after he was shot. Unable to lead from the front anymore, he decided to begin a phased withdrawal. The temporarily crippled, pain-racked captain shouted, "Pull back! I'll cover you!"

Leaning against a tree, he was firing his M14 when two young Marines, who were also wounded, limped over to him. "Go! Go!" he told them. "Leave me alone and move back. That's an order!"

"Skipper, we're not leaving you," one of them said. "You're coming with us." They picked him up, threw his arms around their shoulders, and dragged him toward the rear. But even during the withdrawal, the Marines still had to fight their way back for about 100 meters before both sides quit shooting.

The battered Echo and Hotel Companies retreated to Dai Do, where they evacuated their critically wounded and loaded up on more ammo. After Livingston was carried to a hastily established perimeter, he ordered the corpsmen to tend to all the other casualties first even if he passed out from his wounds. Although he lost plenty of blood, the plucky captain remained lucid and wanted to keep fighting. But he was ordered by his superior officer to join the medevac, so he turned over command of Echo Company to a rookie lieutenant.

"WE STILL HAVE FIGHT IN US!"

Meanwhile, Captain Vargas, of Company G, led his men in an assault at Dinh To where he was wounded for the third time. Refusing to give up, Vargas continued to direct and encourage his embattled unit. When he saw his battalion commander crash to the ground from a serious bullet wound, Vargas disregarded his own pain, dashed through a fire-swept area, scooped up his commander, and carried him to an evacuation point in the rear. Picking up an enemy AK-47, he fired away while helping other wounded men to safety and organizing the battalion's perimeter defense. He was then knocked down a fourth time from an RPG explosion, but still managed to fight on.

Kilometers away, Livingston had been taken to a hospital ship. Because there were so many Marines more critically wounded than he was, he lay on a gurney for five hours before he could be treated. Even though he was in a world of hurt, all the captain could think about was the fate of his men. He ended up undergoing seven operations and needed two months to recover in Hawaii.

After Livingston had been taken off the battlefield, the understrength Marine battalion reorganized and, with help from the Army and Air Force, ultimately defeated a North Vietnamese division and three VC battalions totaling an estimated 8,000 to 10,000 soldiers. Many of the enemy soldiers were among the best the NVA had — experienced, well-trained men using new weapons. In the battle, which lasted three days, the Americans killed an estimated 3,000 to 4,000 foes. Of the 800 Marines who entered the fight, only 220 were not killed or wounded.

Livingston had taken his company and hit the NVA's 320th Division in the gut. Echo and the other companies of the proud 2nd Battalion had driven a superior force from the area, kept the critical Cua Viet River open for American supply boats, protected the base at Dong Ha, and thwarted enemy plans of establishing a new southern foothold.

When Livingston learned of the outcome of the battle, he thought, *Eight hundred Marines against 10,000 NVA? That seems like a fair fight.*

For risking his life above and beyond the call of duty during the Battle of Dai Do, James Livingston was presented the Medal of Honor on May 14, 1970, by President Richard Nixon. "It wasn't because I was a super Marine," Livingston later said of the award. "It was because I was a highly trained Marine."

Captain Jay Vargas also received the Medal of Honor for his heroic actions in that battle. He remained in the Marines for nearly 30 years before retiring in 1992 as a colonel. He then worked with veterans affairs.

Livingston, who rose to the rank of major general, spent more than 33 years in the Marines before joining the business world and doing consulting work. The father of two daughters and three grandchildren, he lives with his wife, Sara, in Mount Pleasant, South Carolina. He wrote a book about his military life called Noble Warrior, published by Zenith Press in 2010.

He said one of the most heartening compliments he received came 40 years after the Battle of Dai Do from a former Marine who was a private first class under Livingston's command in Company E. "You were a tough son of a gun," the ex-Marine told Livingston. "But if it hadn't been for your discipline and training, I wouldn't have made it home, and I wouldn't have become a husband and a father."

LAST MAN STANDING

Army Lieutenant Brian Thacker

As an overpowering enemy force began an all-out assault on an isolated hilltop base, the dwindling number of American and South Vietnamese soldiers, who had put up a valiant resistance, finally caved. No longer able to defend the besieged outpost, the friendlies were left with just one option: retreat.

They began withdrawing out the back side of the base — except for a lone American who chose to stay behind and cover them. Armed with an M16 rifle and carrying a radio, Lieutenant Brian Thacker had volunteered to remain in a courageous attempt to hold off the hard-charging enemy long enough for his comrades to escape.

The brave 25-year-old officer knew there was no way he could stop the massive assault by himself, certainly not with just his weapon. But he believed he could stall the enemy by resorting to the most desperate measure imaginable — by radioing for American heavy artillery to fire directly on his own position.

Once the first round was shot, he would have just seconds to run for his life. One mistake, one miscalculation could spell his doom. The timing had to be perfect. . . . *Otherwise,* he told himself, *if the enemy doesn't get me, the artillery will.*

It was March 31, 1971. Thacker, of Battery A, 1st Battalion, 92nd Artillery, was the leader of a six-man artillery observation team at Firebase 6, a vulnerable hill on a mountain ridge in Kontum Province. Their mission had been to support the 50-man South Vietnamese artillery unit that had been firing on the NVA in the valley below.

The evening before the attack, patrols had reported enemy movement. "We're going to be probed [tested]," the base's South Vietnamese captain told Thacker. "Or worse, we're going to be attacked."

The enemy could overtake this base because there's no infantry to back us up, Thacker thought. *We'll be outnumbered. All we can do is be on alert. Well, we better have a good meal and get ready to fight — whenever that will be.* He set up a rotating four-hour shift for guard duty with his men. After taking the 8 P.M.-to-midnight shift, he went into the sleeping quarters — a rock-covered bunker carved into the side of the hill — and closed his eyes.

He was jarred awake at 5:30 A.M. when his sergeant charged into the bunker and shouted, "Wake up, everybody! We're under attack!"

Thacker, who had been sleeping in a wool nightshirt and a pair of cutoff khakis, jammed his feet into his boots, rustled up the rest of the men, grabbed a grenade launcher, and sprinted out into the dawn.

Soldiers were scrambling to their positions to protect the perimeter. Enemy mortars, automatic weapons fire, grenades, flamethrowers, and RPGs had already killed several friendlies, including three of his own men. *This is not a probe,* he told himself. *They are coming hard at us!*

Thacker secured a radio and called for artillery support from a base that was ten kilometers away. He wanted the first round to burst in the air just to the north of the base. It would be far enough away so that it wouldn't kill anyone, but it would let the enemy know that heavy artillery would soon rain down on them.

After an artillery adjustment, the second round exploded closer toward the invaders, but also near enough to the base that Thacker could hear the pitter-patter of shrapnel hitting the leaves. *Two more adjustments and those rounds will hit their mark,* Thacker thought. But he didn't get the chance to direct the firing of more rounds. The South Vietnamese captain called off the artillery, fearing the shrapnel from the blasts would just as likely rip into his own men as the enemy.

LAST MAN STANDING

The South Vietnamese soldiers and the handful of Americans were forced to defend the base on their own. Their only support came from gunships circling above, strafing the enemy but without enough firepower to keep the large NVA force from streaming toward the firebase.

From his radio, Thacker could hear the pilots' dire reports: "There are twenty moving up the hill!" "We took out three enemy soldiers from a platoon, but the rest have hidden behind the rocks." "They're moving again! There are so many it looks like a whole regiment!"

In the 20 months that he had been an artilleryman, Thacker had never been in a major firefight, but his training and courage directed his actions as if he were a battle-scarred veteran. Taking on the role of a cool, collected field commander, Thacker occupied a dangerously exposed position for hours while directing air strikes and rallying the troops.

As the hours mounted, enemy forces began penetrating the perimeter defenses and engaging the defenders in hand-to-hand combat. Through it all, Thacker continued encouraging his comrades to resist.

A South Vietnamese machine gunner was effectively laying down suppressive fire at the oncoming enemy, trying to break up the advance. RPGs were attacking his position, but they couldn't silence him, mostly because Thacker had deployed two riflemen to protect the gunner.

Midway through the battle, a Huey helicopter swooped in and dropped ammunition, weapons, and other supplies.

But as it was ready to turn and break away, it was hit by a .50-caliber machine gun. To Thacker's horror, the enemy rounds killed the pilot and chewed up the chopper's blades, sending the aircraft crashing into the side of the hill.

Racing to the base's perimeter, Thacker saw the rest of the stunned crew scramble out into the open. Because they looked confused about where to go, he dashed outside the wire and guided them up the hill to relative safety. They had brought their radio but not their machine gun.

When another helicopter came in to pick the airmen up, it also got riddled by the same enemy machine gunner. With its transmission shot out, the chopper appeared destined to crash. The pilot had one chance for a hard landing on the firebase's postage-stamp-size landing zone. If he came up short, he would crash. If he came in too long, he would pitch over the other side of the mountain. Fortunately, the experienced pilot managed to crash-land the severely damaged helicopter, so he and his three crewmen got out safely.

I have seven airmen who are now in the infantry, Thacker thought. *Too bad none thought to bring their weapons with them.* Every attempt to retrieve the helicopters' machine guns and ammo was met with fierce enemy fire. *It's no use,* Thacker thought. *The choppers remain easy targets.*

By the afternoon, Thacker and his comrades were still showing surprisingly strong resistance, fighting like cornered rats. But they were being forced back as their perimeter kept shrinking a bunker at a time because the enemy had superior manpower and firepower.

Thacker asked the South Vietnamese captain, "Can we hold?"

"No," he replied. "We don't have enough men."

"How long can we last?"

"Not long."

"Okay, then we should consider taking away the powder and spiking the tubes." Thacker was suggesting they burn the gunpowder and disable the firebase's light artillery weapons, four 105 howitzers. "If and when the NVA take over the base, they won't be able to use the 105s and powder against us during our withdrawal," Thacker said.

By 4 P.M., pilots in the circling gunships were reporting that a growing number of NVA soldiers were charging the base. "They just keep coming up the hill and we can't stop them," radioed an aviator.

Although the friendlies had burned all the powder, they had run out of time disabling the howitzers. Everyone had to leave now. The surviving defenders' best hope was to run up the spine of the mountain from the base and find a clearing where they could be airlifted to safety before the sun went down. If there was no place for helicopters to land, then the men would have to hustle — and possibly fight their way — to the nearest outpost, Firebase 5, eight kilometers away.

Thacker began organizing and directing the withdrawal. But he had no intention of going with his comrades. "I'll stay inside the wire for as long as I can and provide cover fire," he told the captain.

As the friendlies headed up the ridge, the enemy closed in from the front. The only defenders left were the South Vietnamese machine gunner and Thacker, who had discarded his grenade launcher for an M16 that he had picked up off the ground. He waited until the last possible moment before sending off the gunner and calling in artillery fire on his own position.

Thacker had confidence that he could get out of the blast zone before the shell exploded. "We can't hold our position," he radioed the artillery base. "We are evacuating. I need you to shoot my position . . . and hurry up." He gave the artillery officer the coordinates of Firebase 6.

Thacker was fully aware that the NVA was monitoring his radio channel, just as the friendly forces were monitoring theirs. There were no secrets on the battlefield. Despite the threat of getting bombarded by artillery, the enemy continued advancing. Thacker kept backing up until he was right on the edge of the rear perimeter.

He was waiting for the artillery officer to radio, "Shot!" because that was the signal to run for his life. *Time is running out,* Thacker thought. He radioed the artillery base, "When am I going to hear 'Shot'?"

The artillery officer knew the urgency of the situation and replied, "Get ready to run." Moments later, he ordered Thacker, "Shot! Start moving!".

Thacker abandoned his radio and took off in a sprint. As he scampered up the trail, he calculated how much time he had to make it beyond the bursting radius — a circular area about 200 meters in diameter where the force from the explosion of an artillery shell can kill or injure. He figured he had less than 30 seconds. The machine gunner was already well ahead of him.

Thacker counted to himself . . . *Five seconds . . . ten seconds . . . fifteen seconds . . .* Then it dawned on him that he was totally exposed to the enemy behind him. *Get off the trail!* Suddenly, he heard the boom of the first artillery shot, the sound traveling much slower than the speed of the round. *Four seconds before the shell goes off! You need to find cover! Now!*

Still within the bursting radius, he veered off the trail and scrambled down the mountainside just as the shell exploded in the air with a loud, sharp crack that sent shrapnel whistling in all directions. Thacker fell to the ground to avoid getting struck.

That round was followed by another and another. Over the next 45 minutes, the artillery base fired 38 rounds in an effort to block the enemy from advancing.

Thacker could hear gunfire higher up in the mountain along the trail. It meant that his withdrawing comrades had encountered enemy patrols. Now he had a decision to make: *Do I try to catch up with the others and hope I reach the extraction point — wherever that is — before they are all picked up? Can I get there in time? If I'm late and the choppers are gone, they're not going to come back and look for me. I can't take the chance. I'm better off if I sit it out and hope that the friendlies recapture the firebase.*

That night, Thacker crawled into a brush pile and blended into the side of the mountain. He had no water or food, just his M16 and two magazines. He was still wearing his boots and the clothes he had slept in — his khaki shorts and white wool nightshirt. On edge and on alert, he listened for every little sound, wondering if an NVA patrol was out there looking for any stragglers, any wounded, any soldier like him who hadn't joined the others in the withdrawal. He didn't hear anything. *The NVA doesn't know I'm here, so there's no reason for them to be looking for me,* he thought. Convincing himself that he was relatively safe for the night, he took little catnaps.

The next morning, Thacker realized that the brush pile where he spent the night didn't offer much cover during daylight. He cautiously worked his way farther down the mountain, looking for better protection. When he was about 500 meters away from the firebase, an American A-1 Skyraider, a single-engine, propeller-driven attack plane, flew by. The plane banked sharply and then came back and swooped low. *It's a bombing run!* Thacker realized. Seeing the plane release two bombs, he looked for the closest cover and saw a bamboo thicket. He dived into the thicket, not knowing how big it was or what, if anything, was in it. He curled up in a tiny space no bigger than a small dining room table just as the bombs exploded nearby, showering him in dirt.

The pilot must have spotted movement; maybe it was me or maybe it was the enemy, he thought. *Either way, it's a good sign. The friendlies are monitoring the firebase from the air, which means they're probably going to counterattack.*

As the dust settled, he thought, *This is not a bad place to be. Not enough room to stretch out, but enough to lie down. The Skyraider didn't come back for another run, so I must be pretty well hidden. I think I'll stay here for a while. I feel safe.*

Later that morning, however, he heard voices speaking in Vietnamese and the jangling of military equipment. It was an NVA unit. In an incredible stroke of bad luck, the enemy set up right next to the bamboo thicket where Thacker was hiding. *Oh, oh, this is not good. I'm in the enemy's wire, in the wrong place at the wrong time.* Judging from the sounds, he figured the soldiers were part of an automatic-weapons unit. *They're not here to camp in the woods, so they're here for a reason. It must mean something is going to happen later today.*

He was right. South Vietnamese and American forces counterattacked at 3 P.M. Firefights raged the rest of the day, and bombs from B-52s lit up the sky at night. The NVA unit next to Thacker held a position directly under the approach of American helicopters that were trying to land on the fire-base. *No wonder the enemy set up here,* he thought. *They're trying to shoot down our choppers.*

Thacker spent the night in the thicket, its walls of stalks only a foot thick. Even though the enemy was sometimes within an arm's length of him, he knew bamboo could keep him concealed. As an Air Force brat who spent part of his childhood in Albany, Georgia, he had played hide-and-seek in the backyard where there was a bamboo thicket. If a kid stood in the middle of the thicket, no one could find him — unless someone stuck a stick in there and poked around until he squealed.

By the end of the next day, from what he could hear, Thacker was convinced the friendly forces had driven off the NVA and retaken the base. (They had.) However, the battle was far from over. The enemy kept probing and attacking, but without much success.

Plan A is working, Thacker thought. *But how do I separate from this NVA unit and get up the mountain and back to the firebase? There's no opportunity for separation right now. If I bolt from this thicket, they'll have someone running ten meters behind me, shooting at me. No, I have to be patient.*

He spent another night in his bamboo hideout without food or water. He didn't dare move, knowing the slightest sound could alert the enemy. With no way to quench his thirst or hunger and no way to escape, Thacker was forced to remain in his own self-imposed prison as one insufferable day and night dragged on to the next. He slept lightly, afraid to snore.

To compensate for his lack of seeing what was around him, Thacker's other senses became more acute. He could smell the enemy's body odor and their food. He relied on his hearing the most, especially at night. He listened to the NVA soldiers fixing their meals, cleaning their weapons, and going down to the spring to fill their canteens. They talked in muffled voices and usually communicated by signaling with metal cricket clickers.

To pass the time, Thacker watched the way the bamboo cast shadows during the sun's movement across the sky. From 10 A.M. to 2 P.M., when the sun was directly overhead, he sweated. At night, when it was cool, he kept warm in his wool shirt. Although not religious, he prayed to every god he could think of, including some from mythology.

Thacker, who had been commissioned an officer through ROTC at Weber State University in Utah, knew from his training that he could survive many days without food. There wasn't anything to eat in the thicket anyway, other than an occasional ant or other insect, which he chose not to consume.

Although he could tolerate hunger pangs, thirst was driving him crazy, and he repeatedly fought the urge to sneak out to seek water. There were times when he imagined guzzling a whole lake. He even thought about a cartoon he once saw: Roadrunner slips super-spicy hot sauce to Wile E. Coyote and, with his tongue on fire, Coyote dives into a river and swallows all the water, leaving fish flopping on the dry bottom. Thinking about the cartoon made Thacker envious of Coyote. Back in reality, Thacker didn't expect any rain because it was the dry season in Vietnam, so he was over-joyed when it sprinkled one night. It allowed him to lick moisture off the plants.

His confinement had taken a toll on his body, and he was steadily losing strength. After an unbearable seven days without anything to eat or barely anything to drink, he thought, *How much longer can I stay before my body won't be strong enough to make it out of here? When will I lose all my energy? How far and how fast will I be able to run if I have to?* His body was telling him to leave now.

Thacker decided the best time to slip out would be dur-ing the day, when there were more noises than at night, when every little sound could be heard. Part of the early-morning routine for the NVA unit was to lob mortar rounds at the firebase. After the friendlies fired back, everyone would settle down and have breakfast and carry out their morning chores. *That's when I'm getting out of here,* he told himself.

On the eighth day, Thacker woke up while it was still dark. He strapped on his boots and waited for the enemy to stop its morning mortar attack. He gave them time to put their weapons away and turn their attention to breakfast.

The noises should cover any rustling of the leaves, he told himself. *I just have to sneak out and go about 25 meters, and then I'll be far enough away so they won't hear me. . . . Okay, it's time.*

Because the NVA seldom took prisoners, he knew that if he were discovered, he would likely be executed. Ever so slowly he low-crawled his way out of the thicket . . . five meters . . . ten meters . . . *Rest. Breathe.* The exertion on his weakened body and the mounting tension had taken the breath out of him. *Don't pant! That's a sound that will alert the enemy.* Suppressing the impulse to pant, he took careful, deliberate quiet breaths. Fifteen meters . . . twenty meters . . . *Rest. Breathe.* Twenty-five meters . . . thirty meters . . . *Okay, they can't hear me anymore. Now focus on reaching the firebase.*

He stood up, took a few steps, and rested. Repeating this pattern to save what little energy he had left and to better avoid detection, he walked little by little through the tree line until he came to a clearing at the bottom of the hill. The last 100 meters to the perimeter of the firebase were all in the open. He was now less worried about getting shot by the enemy and more concerned about getting shot by friendlies because he was approaching from an NVA position. *How am I going to cross that final stretch when the friendlies don't know it's me?* he wondered. *If they see movement, they might take me for the enemy. I better not pop out of nowhere, because whoever is standing guard will reflexively shoot at me.*

He low-crawled out from the tree line. Seeing that a guard on the perimeter had his rifle pointed at him, the bearded Thacker slowly stood up, took off his white shirt, and waved it. Other guards appeared. *They have to notice my white skin,* he thought. *This is not the skin of an enemy soldier.*

He exhaled with relief when the guard shouted, "Come on up!" Thacker staggered a few steps, stumbled, and fell on the hillside. He had run out of gas. *I can't go any farther. I'm spent.*

A South Vietnamese soldier ran down, picked up Thacker, and carried him to the top of the hill and inside the wire. Thacker tried to speak — he wanted to say thank you — but all that came out was a croak. His throat and tongue were so parched that he couldn't utter a word.

Weak, dehydrated, and starving, Thacker was brought to a medic, who told him, "Don't try to talk because you could rupture your vocal cords and bleed out."

Because he was in such poor physical condition, Thacker had to be hydrated slowly. Every 15 minutes he was given just a half of a canteen cap of water that was dribbled a drop at a time on his cracked lips and parched tongue. Eventually, he received a few sips of warm milk. Thacker was suffering from a host of health issues from his trial by thirst and starvation. He had lost 30 pounds, his heart was damaged, and his other organs were close to shutting down. Unfortunately, he couldn't get medevacked out right away.

"Glad to have you back, Lieutenant," a major told him later in the day. "But you're creating problems for us. As you know, the enemy monitors our radio networks, and they're really upset that you made it back here. They didn't even know you were out there. So now they aren't going to let you go without a fight. We accept that. It's not the card we want, but we'll play the hand."

Twice a helicopter tried to land, but well-placed mortar rounds prevented that from happening. All the chopper could do was drop supplies to the men and fly away without Thacker.

During another medevac attempt the next day, Thacker was carried out on a stretcher to the pickup zone. Just as the helicopter came in close, the area was mortared, forcing the chopper to back off. Shrapnel from one of the rounds struck Thacker in the arm, but the wound wasn't serious.

Determined to extract Thacker, the pilot made several fake attempts at landing. Each time it looked as if the helicopter was going to touch down, the enemy fired a mortar round and the chopper moved off. However, with expert timing following the last of a series of mortar rounds, the pilot looped around and landed. Within seconds, Thacker was put onboard and the helicopter took off before the next round landed.

Lying on the stretcher and yearning for something to quench his thirst, Thacker squeaked, "Anybody bring a Coke?" One of the crewmen handed him a bottle of Pepsi.

Thacker took a few sips and smiled. Pepsi never tasted so good.

Brian Thacker was taken to the hospital in Pleiku before being transferred to one in Japan. It took more than six months for him to fully recover.

He learned that the withdrawal of his comrades was successful. They didn't even go a mile up the ridge before they found an opening big enough for the choppers to land and get most everyone out. A few Americans went missing in action — including one who had gone back to look for Thacker.

For valor, selfless service, and leadership, Thacker was awarded the Medal of Honor in 1973. After leaving the military, he earned a degree in public health in 1975 at the University of Hawaii and then worked for the U.S. Department of Veterans Affairs for 25 years. Now retired, Thacker lives in Wheaton, Maryland.

"I lost three men up there," Thacker says. "I'm the one who gets to talk about what happened and gets all the glory. There are three grieving mothers whose sons were every bit as brave and had the courage to remain in the firing positions where I wanted them to be. Had they not been there, I wouldn't be here."

GLOSSARY

ACAV armored cavalry assault vehicle

adrenaline a hormone produced by the body that prepares the individual to deal with stress

Agent Orange code name for various chemicals and herbicides that kill plants and trees, depriving the enemy of cover

AK-47 an enemy automatic assault rifle, originally manufactured in the former Soviet Union

ARVN Army of the Republic of Vietnam, allies of the Americans

ASAP abbreviation for "as soon as possible"

AWOL abbreviation for "absent without leave" (or without permission)

GLOSSARY

battalion a military unit of ground forces usually consisting of two or more companies and a headquarters and totaling about 600 to 800 members

battery an artillery company

battle buddies pairs of soldiers who stick together and look out for each other during combat

boat people refugees who fled Vietnam after the fall of Saigon on fishing vessels, rafts, and rickety boats

brigade a military unit consisting of two or more battalions containing 3,500 to 5,000 members

call sign the name and/or number of a combat unit or aircraft used in radio identification

cluster bomb a canister dropped from an aircraft that opens to release a number of small fragmentation explosives over a wide area

commo short for communication

company a military unit typically consisting of several platoons that vary in number according to its mission

contrail the visible condensation of water droplets or ice crystals in the wake of an aircraft, rocket, or missile

cooking off when ammunition explodes prematurely due to heat or fire

corpsman a medically trained enlisted naval person assigned to provide battlefield medical care to Marines or sailors

GLOSSARY

deployment the assignment of military personnel to a tour of duty

division usually consisting of three brigade-size elements, commanded by a major general, and containing 10,000 to 15,000 soldiers

draftee a man required by the Selective Service to serve in the armed services

DUSTOFF the call sign for a medical evacuation from a battlefield by helicopter; also the nickname for the medical evacuation chopper

firefight a battle between ground forces using guns, grenades, and other fired weapons

flak jacket a vest with special material designed to stop fragments from grenades, rockets, and bullets; also called body armor

forward air controller a person who coordinates air strikes

friendlies U.S. troops, allies, or those who aren't the enemy or helping the enemy

Geneva Convention a series of international agreements establishing rules for the humane treatment of prisoners of war, noncombatants, the sick, wounded, and dead in battle

Green Beret a member of the United States Army's Special Forces

grunt slang for infantryman

gunship armed attack aircraft

GLOSSARY

hot dangerous, intense, under fierce enemy fire

in-country military slang for duty in a foreign country

KIA abbreviation for "killed in action"

kill zone an area in a battle where the enemy hopes to kill the most soldiers

kilometer roughly six-tenths of a mile

klick (also spelled click) slang for kilometer

leatherneck slang for Marine

LZ landing zone

M16 the most widely used American military automatic assault rifle

M60 American-made 7.62-mm machine gun

magazine container holding rounds of ammunition that is inserted into a weapon

medevac a term for medical evacuation; a mission flown by helicopters to remove wounded personnel from a battle area

meter slightly more than a yard or roughly three feet, three inches

MIA abbreviation for "missing in action"

MiG Russian-built jet fighter

morphine a strong painkiller

mortar a muzzle-loading, high-angle gun with a short barrel that fires shells at high elevations for a short range

napalm a gelling agent used in bombs that erupt in flames

GLOSSARY

newbie a serviceman or servicewoman who is a recent arrival in country; a rookie, tenderfoot, or greenhorn

NVA North Vietnamese Army

outside the wire beyond the safety of the perimeter; on patrol

perimeter the guarded boundary that forms the outer limits of a military force's position

platoon a small military unit typically consisting of three or more squads of between 20 and 30 persons per squad

POW abbreviation for "prisoner of war"

Purple Heart a U.S. military decoration awarded to members of the armed forces who have been wounded or killed in action

PZ pickup zone for helicopters extracting soldiers from the battlefield

radio traffic the amount of activity broadcast over a communications system

regiment a unit, commanded by a colonel, which is typically bigger than a battalion and smaller than a division

RPG a rocket-propelled grenade launched from a shoulder-fired portable weapon

SAM surface-to-air missile

sapper in Vietnam, an enemy commando trained in explosives

shrapnel fragments from an exploded mine, bomb, or shell

GLOSSARY

Special Forces An elite unit of the United States Army trained for unconventional warfare, reconnaissance, search and rescue, and counterterrorism; known as the Green Berets

spider hole a one-man, hand-dug, camouflaged fighting position used by guerrillas that was often connected to another hole or a tunnel network

squad the smallest military unit typically consisting of 8 to 20 soldiers

suppressive fire a flurry of rounds directed at the enemy to keep them pinned down, preventing them from shooting at moving targets; also called cover fire

tour *or* **tour of duty** a period of time spent assigned to service in a foreign country

tracer round a bullet filled with a flare that burns bright, allowing the shooter to get a better aim on a moving target

troop another name for a soldier or group of soldiers; also a company-size armored cavalry

turret a self-contained weapons platform housing guns on a vehicle and capable of rotation

Viet Cong term for Vietnamese communist guerilla or guerilla forces fighting the South Vietnamese government and American troops; often called VC for short or nicknamed "Charlie"

ABOUT THE AUTHOR

Allan Zullo is the author of more than 100 nonfiction books on subjects ranging from sports and the supernatural to history and animals.

He has introduced Scholastic readers to the *Ten True Tales* series, gripping stories of extraordinary persons who have met the challenges of dangerous, sometimes life-threatening, situations. Among the books in the series are *FBI Heroes, Heroes of 9/11, World War II Heroes, War Heroes: Voices from Iraq,* and *Battle Heroes: Voices from Afghanistan.* In addition, he has authored four books about the real-life experiences of young people during the Holocaust — *Survivors: True Stories of Children in the Holocaust, Heroes of the Holocaust: True Stories of Rescues by Teens, Escape: Children of the Holocaust,* and *We Fought Back: Teen Resisters of the Holocaust.*

Allan, the father of two grown daughters and grandfather of five, lives with his wife, Kathryn, near Asheville, North Carolina. To learn more about the author, visit his website at www.allanzullo.com.